PRAISE FOR
SIX STEPS TO FREE PUBLICITY

"The most comprehensive single source for solid, clear, and immediately useful advice."
> —Alan Weiss, author of
> *Million Dollar Consulting*

"Discover how to unleash the power of publicity to help sell your products, services or yourself. With this step-by-step, do-it-yourself guide, you'll profit from free media coverage— just like the pros do."
> —Frank Grazian, executive editor,
> *Communications Briefings*

"Yudkin proves that in business, as in life, many of the best things are free. I predict this will be the most used book in any self-promoter's library."
> —Barbara Winter, author of
> *Making a Living Without a Job*

"This marvelous book is jammed with tremendous ideas which will obtain gigantic sales for whatever you wish to sell. I couldn't put it down!"
> —Dottie Walters, publisher/editor,
> *Sharing Ideas Newsmagazine for*
> *Professional Speakers*

MARCIA YUDKIN is a writer, consultant, and seminar leader who provides fresh perspectives on communicating creatively. Her articles have appeared in magazines ranging from the *New York Times Magazine* and *Psychology Today* to *Ladies' Home Journal* and *Cosmopolitan*. She is the co-author, with Laurie Schloff, of *Smart Speaking* and *He and She Talk*, and the author of *Freelance Writing for Magazines and Newspapers*.

"Packed full of great ideas and information, this book is an important resource for artists and arts organizations. It demystifies the puzzle of who receives publicity and why!"
—Carroll Michels, author of
*How to Survive and
Prosper as an Artist*

"Marcia Yudkin gives the kind of advice you can sit down and start using right away! *Six Steps to Free Publicity* takes you from feeling like 'who me' to saying 'and how!' If you run a business, read this book."
—Alice Bredin, Prodigy home
start-up expert, American Public Radio
commentator, and *Newsday*
"Working at Home" columnist

"A terrific guide for entrepreneurs on how to use creativity instead of cash to generate high-impact marketing results."
—Terri Lonier,
author of *Working Solo*

Also by Marcia Yudkin

Freelance Writing for Magazines and Newspapers
He and She Talk (with Laurie Schloff)
Smart Speaking (with Laurie Schloff)

6

STEPS TO

FREE

PUBLICITY

AND
DOZENS OF OTHER WAYS
TO WIN FREE MEDIA
ATTENTION FOR YOU
OR YOUR BUSINESS

MARCIA YUDKIN

A PLUME BOOK

PLUME
Published by the Penguin Group
Penguin Books USA Inc., 375 Hudson Street,
New York, New York 10014, U.S.A.
Penguin Books Ltd, 27 Wrights Lane,
London W8 5TZ, England
Penguin Books Australia Ltd, Ringwood,
Victoria, Australia
Penguin Books Canada Ltd, 10 Alcorn Avenue,
Toronto, Ontario, Canada M4V 3B2
Penguin Books (N.Z.) Ltd, 182-190 Wairau Road,
Auckland 10, New Zealand

Penguin Books Ltd, Registered Offices:
Harmondsworth, Middlesex, England

First published by Plume, an imprint of Dutton Signet,
a division of Penguin Books USA Inc.

First Printing, October, 1994
10 9 8 7 6 5 4 3 2

 REGISTERED TRADEMARK—MARCA REGISTRADA

LIBRARY OF CONGRESS CATALOGING-IN-PUBLICATION DATA

Yudkin, Marcia.
  Six steps to free publicity : and dozens of other ways to win free media attention for
you or your business / Marcia Yudkin.
      p.   cm.
  ISBN 0-452-27192-4
  1. Publicity   2. Press releases   3. Public relations—Small business.   I. Title.
HD59.Y83   1994
659—dc20   94-13410
                                                                              CIP

Printed in the United States of America
Set in Century Book
Designed by Leonard Telesca

BOOKS ARE AVAILABLE AT QUANTITY DISCOUNTS WHEN USED TO PROMOTE PRODUCTS OR SERVICES. FOR
INFORMATION PLEASE WRITE TO PREMIUM MARKETING DIVISION, PENGUIN BOOKS USA INC., 375 HUDSON
STREET, NEW YORK, NEW YORK 10014.

to Chen,
for challenges and inspiration

Acknowledgments

Most of all, I'd like to thank the editors of *Bottom Line/ Personal*, who printed an offer for the four-page version of *Six Steps to Free Publicity* that lay the groundwork for this book. Special thanks as well to Deb Brody and Diana Finch for their midwifing of the book; Amy Hoberman for enthusiastic research assistance; Jennifer Starr for helpful conversations on entrepreneurship; my sister JJ for ongoing legal advice; my sister Gila for her rigorous feedback; and my mother, Florence, for being the best press agent a daughter could have. Finally, I believe we're all the richer for the insightful, gracious contributions of the people who are quoted herein. Thanks especially to interviewees, too numerous to name, who helped ensure the accuracy of the text.

Contents

GETTING
STARTED
WITH
PUBLICITY

CHAPTER 1

Riches . . . Credibility . . . Prestige . . . Opportunity— What Publicity Can Do for You

On September 13, 1990, I settled into a middle seat on board a USAir flight to San Francisco, trying to keep my excited glow from irking half-awake fellow passengers. A silver-haired woman arranged pillows on the aisle seat and started a conversation. Her third question punctured my restraint.

"I'm a writer and a writing consultant," I replied, and nodded toward a flight attendant who was passing out newspapers. "My partner and I have a company called WordRight. We're in the *Wall Street Journal* today."

She tilted her head sideways. Her eyes widened.

"Page one," I added, allowing myself a grin.

We got up to let by a well-scrubbed man who took off his shoes and introduced himself as a congressman from San Diego. As if matching that, my new acquaintance jerked a thumb at me. "This lady here is in today's *Wall Street Journal.*"

At his look of respect, a little more pride seeped into my smile, and after our seatmate had closed her eyes, I traded stories and experiences with the congressman for most of the flight.

Media publicity can do a lot more for you than feed your ego and enable you to impress strangers on airplanes.

• *Publicity can sell your products or services without the burdensome expense of advertising.* The makers of the game Trivial Pursuit had no advertising budget whatsoever. Instead, by sending sample games or just the cards to game-industry buyers, celebrities who were mentioned in the game, and disk jockeys, they created a stir that the media had to keep reporting. Consequently, sales reached 1.5 million in 1983, the year the game was introduced. That same year, the *Wall Street Journal* ran a feature article about the "streetfighter marketing" ideas of Jeff Slutsky, who ran a one-man consulting business out of his home. "The day the article came out, my phone started ringing at six A.M." he recalls. "It literally didn't stop until ten P.M., and I got a steady flow of calls from that article for three years." Slutsky's free publicity translated into $50,000 of product sales in the first ninety days "—and big clients," he adds.

• *Publicity helps you rise above your competition.* The more media appearances you rack up, the more *your* name comes to mind when people think "pediatrician" or "dating for nerds." The effect keeps building on itself in a three-stage cycle: You earn publicity by setting yourself apart from the competition; then it gives you a higher profile; then, feeling better about yourself, you easily make yourself still more visible. "It's a terrific confidence booster," says Steve Schiffman, a New York City sales trainer whose fifteen years of publicity add up to his getting recognized on the street. "You develop poise and learn how to handle difficult questions. If you do radio and TV regularly, you can cope with anything."

• *Publicity bestows lucrative credibility.* Media appearances greatly boost the perceived value of whatever you offer the public. When Boston actor Norman George sends out a full-page feature story from *People* magazine about him playing Edgar Allan Poe, theaters and cultural organizations take him seriously. Linda Barbanel, a New York City therapist who specializes in the psychology of money, says that the cumulative effect of her 600-plus-and-rising media appearances has been a quadrupling of her speaking fees.

• *Publicity can create profitable, unexpected opportunities.* A question-and-answer feature about my work on creativity in the Sunday *Boston Globe* business section prompted Horizon Media in nearby Quincy to call and ask if I would be interested in collaborating on videos about creativity. "Yes!" I said to this proposal that I would not have thought up on my own. By the time you read this, we will have released three training videos, *What, Me Creative? Eureka! Inspiration and Creativity,* and *Ideas on the Beach.* Half a year after the *Globe* piece, a six-line notice that cost me nothing in the newsletter *Bottom Line/ Personal* led to my contract for this book. (More about this later.)

• *Publicity can crown you as an expert.* After Debbi Karpowicz promoted her humor book, *I Love Men in Tasseled Loafers,* on TV and radio stations, she was invited back as a dating expert. Because, as she puts it, her book chronicles dating disasters from the standpoint of a woman who loves shoes, the media also treated her as an expert on footwear. Similarly, when Claire McCarthy, a communication consultant in North Andover, Massachusetts, promoted a workshop she was offering called "How to Write a Love Letter," the *Lawrence Eagle-Tribune* ran a three-quarter-page profile of her and she received two write-ups in the *Boston Herald.* Even though the workshop never received enough registrants to run, the coverage prompted *North Shore* magazine to interview McCarthy as a romance expert.

• *Publicity can give potential clients a long, close look at you.* Merle Bombardieri, a clinical social worker in Lexington, Massachusetts, knows that her TV appearances have prompted people who needed counseling to call her. "Sometimes they had already heard of me, but people find it difficult to open their hearts to a perfect stranger," Bombardieri says. "They're afraid that a therapist might be judgmental or arrogant. But when they see someone on TV they get a sense of that person's personality and style. Several people who saw me on TV said that I seemed like an intelligent, approachable person with a sense of humor, and that made it much easier for them to call."

• *Publicity often rallies public support to your cause.* Publicity literally saves lives when people who need organ transplants or the means to pay for them have their cases dramatized to millions on the air or in print. On a bigger scale, massive media coverage contributed to one million people participating in the first annual Take Our Daughters to Work Day on April 28, 1993. Through roughly 5,000 print articles and countless radio and TV stories, hundreds of millions of people who did not participate were exposed to its goal of increasing the self-esteem and career awareness of adolescent girls. Though the event had some detractors, particularly those worried about the boys who had been left out for one day, organizers soon heard from schools and employers eager to prepare their participation for the following year.

• *Publicity for good works earns you community goodwill.* For fifteen years after founding The Body Shop, Anita Roddick abstained from any advertising for her natural cosmetics. Instead, she attracted mounds of media attention because of her environmental and social activism. One project of hers, "Trade, Not Aid," helps native cultures around the world to prosper by growing ingredients for her cosmetics. Roddick has also organized a campaign to refurbish Romanian orphanages and another for voter registration. In 1990, The Body Shop estimated that it was receiving about $3.5 million a year in free publicity. People who admire her passionate stands "understand that purchases support a good cause," observed *Working Woman*, "and as a result are more likely to buy."

• *Publicity has the power to counteract stereotypes.* When I visited Taos Pueblo not long ago, I noticed and read a newspaper clipping framed on a shop wall about a Pueblo man making language videos for the tribe's young people. "Is this you?" I asked the shopkeeper, a silversmith. "My brother," he said. The conversation started by that clipping, during which I learned that the silversmith had studied dentistry at Harvard, opened my eyes about the sort of people who would choose to live and work in a traditional Native American setting. Similarly, articles in the Boston media about Empire Loan, a pawnshop, relieved me of the notion that only seedy, unshaven characters, thieves, and heiresses who had overspent their trust fund frequented pawnshops.

• *Publicity gets your message across in a seemingly objective manner.* In 1980, *Wall Street Journal* executive editor Frederick Taylor admitted that as much as 90 percent of its daily news originates in self-interested press releases. Yet when the public reads what reporters have done with that information, it tends to trust and respect the material, which rarely happens with advertising. Breakthrough Software Corporation received dramatic proof of this credibility difference in 1985, when it spent $6,000 to advertise one of its programs and received 100 responses. A free favorable magazine review of the same program, however, generated 900 responses. Some media mentions, such as on the front page of the newspaper, can't be bought for any price.

• *Publicity may make you eligible for professional recognition.* To earn the designation "Professional Member" in the Association of Image Consultants International, among many other requirements you have to have received media publicity. In the classical music world, organizations that award grants to community music groups take local media coverage as an important sign of community impact and interest. Not only do the grants bestow prestige, they often spell the difference between financial survival and failure. For scientists and medical researchers, media coverage leads to more citations by other scientists, sometimes used as a measure of professional impact in decisions on hiring and promotion. A 1991 study revealed that research covered in the *New York Times* as well as in the *New England Journal of Medicine* received 73 percent more scholarly citations the next year than research reported only in the *New England Journal of Medicine.*

• *Publicity can provide the occasion for outrageous fun.* Providence, Rhode Island, entertainer Ron Bianco recalls sitting in his kitchen laughing out loud while he was planning a 1988 campaign to run his dog Bilbo, who was part of his folksinging act, for president. In Broad Brook, Connecticut, John Collins found a way to attract attention and have a blast with his otherwise unremarkable fledgling business of recycling toner cartridges from laser printers. A tongue-in-cheek article in his local paper, the *Journal Inquirer,* carried the headline IT'S A BIRD, IT'S A PLANE . . . NO, IT'S TONER MAN! and showed him in a Superman-like costume. An employee said that Collins's appearances as Toner Man helped relieve stress on the job.

In today's economic climate, shooting for free media coverage makes especially good sense. Rochester, New York, consultant and author Harvey Kaye says that forty years ago, engineers were such a small percentage of the population that people who needed their services sought them out. His father, a professor at MIT, never had to do any marketing. Today, however, so many technical experts crowd the market that if they don't promote themselves, he says, it's career suicide. The same goes for therapists, restaurant owners, graphic artists, hairdressers, accountants, and most others in business for themselves. The old saying, "Build a better mousetrap and the world will beat a path to your door," is not true today, if it ever was. People first need to know about your door from advertising or its cheaper and more credible alternative, publicity.

Publicity costs you nothing but time and energy and, sometimes, money for copying and postage. Even better, you don't need a degree in public relations to receive the benefits enumerated above. *Six Steps to Free Publicity* takes you step by step through the process, including finding a hook that will snag the interest of the media, writing or calling them, doing your best to ensure that your message gets through to the appropriate audience, and cementing relationships that enhance your opportunities for repeated media exposure. In the coming chapters you'll learn:

- How to strategize about the appropriate goals, focus, and target audience for your publicity efforts.
- Why publicity doesn't necessarily involve hype, and how to find the method of gaining publicity that feels most comfortable for you.
- How to write, format, and send a press release that has the best chance of resulting in media coverage.
- Other ways to attract the interest of the media, such as making a phone pitch, writing letters to reporters and editors, and staging unique events.
- How to spread word of mouth by neatly encapsulating your message, getting friendly with the press, and being memorable.
- The do's and don'ts of dealing with reporters, producers, and other media folks.
- How to perform on radio or TV like a pro.

- Ways to come up with creative publicity approaches and carve out the time to execute them, as well as
- How to go beyond what Andy Warhol called everyone's "fifteen minutes of fame" to a lasting media presence for you, your business, or your cause.

Throughout the book you'll encounter examples of real people who used the methods I'll be describing to get their word out. I've concentrated on low-cost, high-impact strategies that most reasonably motivated, ordinary mortals might be able to pull off. Don't worry if you sometimes have the reaction while reading of other people's exploits, "I could never do *that.*" I've included enough different approaches that you're bound to discover some that feel right for you. And since no one emerges from the womb knowing how to land media coverage, you'll find nitty-gritty advice for each aspect of the process.

Although publicity can launch you toward fame, influence, and fortune, it will not offer a magic carpet ride for everyone, every time. Its uncontrollability can be a problem, but also an advantage. I couldn't possibly have known the afternoon I mailed hundreds of press releases about a catchy new business service that the Gulf War would break out overnight and drive all otherwise newsworthy stories out of reporters' minds. On the other hand, who would have guessed that a simple letter and sample copy of a newsletter would have led to a piece in the *Maine Sunday Telegram* about the *Tightwad Gazette*, through that to an article in *Parade*, and through that to a contract for a book by the same title that reached national bestseller lists?

Publicity-seeking might be called an adventure except that, unlike hunting elephants, it holds few dangers. Rarely does publicity backfire, and rarely will a series of intelligently conceived, knowledgeably executed publicity campaigns totally fail. And you won't have to practice for years before you reap rewards. By following the guidelines in this book, inventor Sandra Weintraub wrote her first press release ever and attracted the attention of *Mirabella*, Australian *Vogue*, *Allure*, and the *Wall Street Journal* for her "Harasser Flasher" pin, designed to curtail sexual harassment. So let's get started now with the questions and perspectives that can get you thinking like a publicity hound.

CHAPTER 2

Thinking Like
a Publicity Hound

Suppose you're opening a new branch of your hardware store in Cactus Junction, Texas, population 21,500, 158 miles southwest of Dallas. Cash flow is one way so far, and you've heard that publicity is the low-cost alternative to advertising, so you contact every newspaper in Texas with your announcement, printed up in classy italic type at your local print shop. For good measure, you throw in all the NBC, ABC, and CBS affiliate stations from El Paso to Texarkana, and National Public Radio in Austin.

For a prosaic local store opening, does that sound to you like a wise expenditure of effort?

Since I deliberately chose an extreme example, you're probably shaking your head.

Effective publicity involves a match between your goals and the needs of the media. Without considering what you hope to achieve from publicity, you're unlikely to receive an optimal outcome. And unless you take into account what the media want to cover, you might as well have addressed your materials to a black hole. The best place to begin your quest for publicity is with a frank, dispassionate assessment of the results you would most benefit from.

Getting Clear on Your Goals

Use the following checklist to zero in on your specific needs and wants.

1. *Which of the following do you want most—credibility and prestige; customers, clients, donors, or attendees; changed or opened minds?* It's all right to want it all, but the long-range aim of establishing your reputation as a trombone player may require you to target different media outlets and choose different tactics than the short-term goal of selling out the hall at your recital next month. A campaign to enhance your musical reputation can be sporadic and diffuse, as can a crusade to change the image of the trombone, but a push to sell tickets must reach the concertgoing audience at the appropriate time and place with accurate information about the performance. Articulating your priorities is fundamental to any successful publicity venture.

2. *Where, geographically, does it make sense for you to aim—nationally, regionally, or locally?* If you're opening a new hardware store, you need to recognize that few people will drive hundreds of miles, or even a dozen miles, if alternatives exist, to buy nails. If your operation included a nails-by-mail program, on the other hand, regional and national publicity could yield customers. Don't let the glamour and glitter of famous media outlets and huge audiences blind you to your need to focus where your prospects live—in this case, right in and around Cactus Junction.

3. *Who, specifically, are you hoping to reach?* A consultant friend of mine hired a public relations firm to get her media exposure. After some months they announced that they'd booked her on a national TV talk show. Instead of whooping for joy, my friend asked when the show ran. Because the show aired in the afternoon, she declined the opportunity. Her target audience was corporate executives, and how many of them watch the tube in the daytime? Once you know that you're trying to get your story to, say, sofa manufacturers east of the Mississippi, men who are self-conscious about going bald, or potential fur

buyers with a social conscience, you can concentrate on the media outlets they read, listen to, and watch.

4. *Are you hoping to sell a particular product?* If so, then persuading, cajoling, and even begging the media to include contact information—your address and/or phone number—is crucial. According to Cambridge, Massachusetts, publisher Jeffrey Lant, most entrepreneurs greatly overestimate the willingness of consumers to go to a lot of trouble to order something. If getting in touch with you requires anything more complicated than a call to local directory information, most people won't bother. Consequently, Lant insists on his address or phone number being published or broadcast (you can find it in Chapter 23) whenever he appears in print or on the air.

Not everyone agrees with Lant's reasoning, however. Greg Godek, who self-published *1001 Ways to Be Romantic* and *1001 More Ways to Be Romantic* under the imprint of Casablanca Press, says his main concern during media appearances is to build up his image as "America's Number-One Romantic." Godek believes that implanting that image in the public's mind will result in more sales over the long run than would a short-term fixation on selling a certain number of books each time he goes on the air or shows up in print. Whether or not he's right, as part of your strategizing you ought to ask yourself how much maintaining a certain image matters to you. Your answer should affect your thinking on my next question as well.

5. *Will you welcome any and all publicity opportunities, or will you want to pick and choose among opportunities to maintain a certain image and focus?* Because of his image-building strategy, Greg Godek found himself in the unusual position of persuading a producer of the Oprah Winfrey show not to book him. When Oprah's producer invited him to appear on a show about sex, Godek carefully explained that anything he would have to say would come from the slant of romance, and after a long discussion, the producer agreed that he was not right for that show. "I could tell she was impressed," Godek says, "because most people would do anything to get on Oprah. That puts me in a better position to get on when the topic is right for me. I'm convinced that if people don't see you as you really are, it won't help you."

Likewise, Tony Putman, a marketing consultant in Ann Arbor,

Michigan, shies away from newspaper publicity because he's afraid they'll mistakenly position him as an advertising guru. "That would be damaging to my public image," says Putman, who in fact stresses other means of marketing besides advertising for service businesses. Although I think there's much you can do to ensure that reporters get your point (see Chapter 14), I agree that it's a good idea to consider whether some media might be irrelevant to or inconsistent with your goals. For example, since my market tends to be better-educated people and I offer serious professional services and products, I wouldn't get excited about a chance to appear in the *National Enquirer* or *Penthouse*.

6. *Do you have reason to lean more to one medium than another?* The tangibility and relative permanence of print make it ideal for many publicity-seekers, but if you were, say, a comic entertainer, your preferences might run like this: most helpful, TV; next, radio; next, newspaper or magazine article with a photo; least helpful, an article without a photo. Or if you're a high-energy, high-personal-impact salesman, you might feel that the hotter electronic media capture your essence best.

The Key That Unlocks Media Doors

Once you settle your priorities, you can turn to the other half of the match that produces effective publicity, namely, what interests the media. Here the crux is understanding the fundamental question in the mind of any editor, reporter, or producer: *Why would our readers (or listeners or viewers) be interested in this story now?*

This fundamental question breaks down into three essential parts. If you present your case to the media in a way that speaks to all three concerns, you'll come as close to guaranteed coverage as any law-abiding citizen can. First comes "our readers/listeners/viewers." Every media outlet from *Business Week* or *CBS This Morning* to *Ski Area Management* or *The New Age News Hour* has an audience profile and an editorial mission that determine what does and doesn't fall within its scope of coverage. If the audience your media pitch appeals to resembles the audience of that outlet, so far so good. You meet this requirement partly by choosing your target media intelligently and partly by being explicit about what connects you or your business or organization with a particular audience. Send something to *Ski Area Management* headlined HEALTH PROFESSIONALS OFFER FREE SEMINARS and they'll toss your materials out, but change the headline to VERMONT CHIROPRACTOR GROUP OFFERS FREE, ENTERTAINING SEMINARS ON PREVENTIVE BACK CARE AT SKI RESORTS and they'll pay close attention.

Second comes "this story." Yours had better be a short, focused story, not an endless saga. Stick to one main point each time you approach the media. Instead of saying, "Your readers might want to know how I rose from poverty, conquered cancer, recently sold my shoe repair shop, and patented an automatic bird feeder," talk about how you got off welfare while raising seven kids alone *or* how you recovered from your doctors' death sentence through experimental surgery *or* how you sold Sole Mate to an Italian chain *or* how your new device makes birdseed accessible to bluebirds but not blue jays. If you've got so much claim on public attention, spread your stories out over several campaigns.

Journalists call your choice of focus the "hook" or the "angle" of a story, and it does the job insofar as it addresses the third and paramount concern of media people, "now." What makes your story timely? Or, how can you inject timeliness into your story? You can give yourself a crash course on newsworthiness by reading newspaper features or listening carefully to non–lead news items, asking yourself what makes each story relevant now. As America braced for the release of the film *Jurassic Park*, for instance, both National Public Radio and ABC News aired reports about a man named Donald Bean who had created a theme park in Moscow, Texas, called Dinosaur Gardens. Bean had opened the park years before, but the impending arrival of a blockbuster film on dinosaurs had elevated anything to do with dinosaurs to relevance.

Devoting careful thought to timeliness will make your publicity efforts pay off. In many cases, it's worth inventing a sideline service, event, or unusual characterization of what you do to entice the media to spread the word about you. To generate ideas, use the following checklist of ways to provide a compelling "now" for editors and producers.

Ten Ways to Be Timely

1. *What is new about your business or organization?* What's new might include anything from just opening shop to promoting someone within your organization. Consider any or all of the following as excuses for getting into print:

- Just opening. Properly approached, *The Cactus Junction Gazette* would probably gladly run a free notice about your hardware store opening.
- Posting record quarterly profits, receiving a grant, capturing a more favorable market share, lowering prices, surpassing previous years' donations, hiring or promoting people, giving recognition awards, renaming the company, relocating, and other organizational news.
- Offering new services or programs, serving new areas or populations.
- Releasing new products or new versions of products.

Contacting appropriate media three or four times a year with the above kinds of announcements would not be too much. The *Wall Street Journal* isn't alone in relying on unsolicited information. Hometown newspapers and trade magazines couldn't fill their pages without receiving seemingly mundane notices from people like you. You'll get the best results by combining this strategy with one of those that follow, but remember, if you don't tell the press what you're doing, who will?

2. *What is different or distinctive about your business or organization?* If your dry-cleaning establishment is Tibetan-owned and operated, that's news. If you use your Ph.D. in sociology to study home cleanliness while you clean houses, that's news. If your counseling service specializes in helping people who are HIV-positive, that's certainly mediaworthy. Kim Merritt of Cumberland, Maryland, was only sixteen years old, though an experienced chocolate maker, when she took on the

project of producing 18,000 candy bars for her high school's annual fund-raising drive. For fun, she wrote about what she was doing to editors at more than a dozen magazines she was familiar with, such as *Teen*, *Cosmopolitan*, and *Good Housekeeping*. Both *People* and *Ms.* magazine bit, and the national publicity that continued to come her way for years helped her specialty chocolate business, Kim's Khocolate, thrive. In 1993 Merritt was twenty-five years old and still using her age as a hook. "Even when I'm eighty the story of how I got started will interest people," she laughs.

Here is where thinking like a publicity hound gives you the chance to set yourself apart from the competition and turn a ho-hum product or service into something newsworthy. Because my partner and I at WordRight knew that the editing services we offered had little publicity value, we added an extra attraction, overnight editing by fax, concocted a name, WordRight Express Editing, and started a promotional blitz. The material I wrote, headlined NEW NATIONAL OVERNIGHT EDITING SERVICE, not only earned us press from Massachusetts to Alaska, it also caught the eye of business guru Tom Peters, who quoted from it and discussed it in his book *Liberation Management*. More recently, I produced an audiotape on procrastination and then decided that the audiotape format had zero publicity potential. By mulling over what might be an innovative format, I invented what I call a "postcard seminar"—participants receive ten weekly oversize postcards, each containing food for thought and a brief exercise adapted from the audiotape. So far as I know, I'm the first to deliver transformational material on a series of postcards—and that definitely sets me apart from other experts and seminar leaders.

3. *Do you have an event you could create or publicize?* As you'll learn in Chapter 10 on "magnet events," occasions that tempt the media to cover you can be quite creative and require a lot of work to organize and pull off. However, events can also be as simple as giving away free samples Saturday from noon to two on Main Street, holding auditions for your company's Talent Show of the Century, or presenting a lecture at the public library. For the media, events transform business as usual into something that can be announced, witnessed, and reported on at a specific time and place. Remember that the more colorful or

visual your event, the more likely it is that you'll be able to draw photographers and TV cameras.

4. *Can you make your products or expertise relevant by piggybacking on current news?* A smart career counselor in search of clients would keep one eye peeled for any change in unemployment statistics. If more people were finding jobs, the up-to-the-minute hook would be "How Not to Be Left Behind in the Current Rehiring," while if joblessness stayed the same or worsened, the timely pitch might be "Microtargeted Résumés Win Jobs Despite Hiring Lull." The connection can be much more distant or unexpected. If a hurricane devastates Louisiana, an insurance agent in Oregon can release a set of tips on how to make sure you're covered in case of a disaster. A marriage therapist might draw some lessons for the public from the latest spat between Princess Di and the Prince of Wales. A restaurant might use newly released statistics about the prevalence of high cholesterol levels as an occasion to tout its healthful menus.

Some of the best opportunities exist when an event, such as a natural disaster or a pending political change, lingers on the front pages for more than a few days. Reporters become desperate for a fresh and sometimes oblique angle on the story. For example, as the Midwest Flood of '93 slogged on, the *Boston Globe* ran a piece on whether the *Farmer's Almanac* or its rival publication, the *Old Farmer's Almanac*, had foretold the disaster accurately. When the battle between Woody Allen and Mia Farrow continued to rage, I noticed collateral stories on celebrities as parents and on adoption. Experienced publicity hounds are constantly sniffing out these sorts of opportunities.

5. *Have you done or could you do some research to merit press coverage?* The American Association of University Women has landed on the front pages and national news broadcasts numerous times by commissioning formal studies on the barriers girls and women experience in schools and colleges. Its findings reached millions more through humorous treatments in more than a dozen comic strips, including "Nancy," "Peanuts," and "Doonesbury." Yet you can receive media attention for informal polls or surveys that wouldn't meet scientific standards. Alan Weiss, president of Summit Consulting Group, Inc., in East Greenwich, Rhode Island, distributed brief questionnaires to newspaper employees about whether they felt underpaid and

whether management was honest with them. The results appeared in *Editor and Publisher*, where key prospects for his consulting services read the story. You could simply ask for a show of hands while speaking at your Rotary Club and write up the tally as LOCAL EXECUTIVES REVEAL THEIR BIGGEST DAILY ANNOYANCE—INTERRUPTERS, and lead into advice from your booklets on time management.

6. *Could you sponsor an interesting contest or award?* Any contest gives you two excuses for publicity: one to announce the contest and the other to reveal the winners. Try to make it more creative than a raffle. Pauline Bartel of Waterford, New York, launched a *"Gone With the Wind* Trivia Contest" at a nearby bookstore to promote her book, *The Complete* Gone With the Wind *Trivia Book*. When the contest was long over, she wrote about her experience in the *Freelance Writer's Report*, where I read about it. Joe Killoran, who publishes a newsletter called *The Frugal Bugle* for Canadian tightwads, issued a public challenge to haggle a copy of the book the *Tightwad Gazette* from a bookseller for far less than list price. Another time he dared readers to come up with a way of buying postal stamps at a discount. In Canada that's possible, and the contest earned him free publicity in the *Financial Post*.

To give an award, you don't have to deal with entries, only select and announce a recipient. For years Senator William Proxmire of Wisconsin made media hay out of his Golden Fleece Award, bestowed on a project that flagrantly (in his mind, at least) wasted taxpayer money. Gary Blake of the Communication Workshop in New York City made up something called the Percy Award, named after the pompous phrase that clutters too many letters, "pursuant to your request." His comments on the worst examples of poor writing he could find appeared on radio stations and in newspapers across the country, including *USA Today*. "They helped my image as a crusader for good writing," he says.

7. *Is there a holiday or anniversary that you could hook onto?* Sure you know about Father's Day and National Secretaries Week, but what about Humpback Whale Awareness Month? Carpet Care Improvement Week? National Cheer Up the Lonely Day? Made in America Month? The bible of special days, weeks, and months is a work called *Chase's Annual Events*,

available in most public libraries. Until I took a close look at it recently, I didn't realize that many of its entries were sponsored—that is, invented—by individuals, companies, and organizations. For example, National Bathroom Reading Week originated with Red-Letter Press, which publishes twenty-one different books especially designed for bathroom reading. Relationship Renewal Day came into existence when therapist Peter Rosenzweig thought it up as a way to plug his book, *Married and Alone: The Way Back.* All you need to do to get your catchy creation included in *Chase's* is to submit your information according to the instructions at the back of the volume. Even if you do no other promotion, you could still be deluged with media inquiries from around the world, says Ruth Roy, a sponsor of Stay Home Because You're Well Day.

Just a half hour with *Chase's* should spark plenty of ideas for taking advantage of existing occasions. Mental health and alcohol counselor Szifra Birke of Chelmsford, Massachusetts, organized and promoted a kids' poster contest for National Children of Alcoholics Week. The contest was covered three times by the *Lowell Sun,* as well as in the *Boston Globe* and two other area newspapers. One of my writing students brought to class a clipping from the *Globe* that started off TODAY IS TUESDAY OF NATIONAL GET ORGANIZED WEEK and listed tips from Barbara Hemphill, a board member of the National Association of Professional Organizers.

Of course, don't overlook traditional holidays or well-known anniversaries. Many publications and shows eagerly embrace novel story ideas in connection with, say, Veterans Day or Martin Luther King Day. If you provide legal advice for ex-servicepeople or founded a racial harmony community program, those are the times to let the media know. Greg Godek, author of the *1001 Ways to Be Romantic* books, concentrates so intensely on publicity as the clock ticks down to February 14 that on Valentine's Day he's giving interviews for practically twenty-four hours straight. Communication consultant Laurie Schloff remembers that in 1965, she and her thirteen-year-old friends received coverage in the *Elizabeth Daily Journal* in New Jersey for their celebration of the first anniversary of the Beatles' arrival in America.

8. *Is there a trend in the general population or some particular population that relates to your offerings?* Here you borrow timeliness from general currents that drift through society rather than from the headlines. According to Kim Merritt, in the mid-eighties entrepreneurship was such a hot topic that the Association of Collegiate Entrepreneurs was getting two to three unsolicited calls from the press every day. In the nineties, "cocooning" (staying home for entertainment), thriftiness, environmental awareness, and embarking on one's fourth career became trends that provided publicity opportunities for many people.

9. *Can you suggest a surprising twist on received opinion?* Jim Cooke, a Boston actor, faced a challenge when he began to portray Calvin Coolidge in a one-man show. "No one is out there holding a meeting saying, 'Let's bring Calvin Coolidge in,' " he says. Since the stereotype of "Silent Cal" is that he said nothing, Cooke drummed up media interest by demonstrating that Coolidge had a sense of humor, held more press conferences than any other president, and was one of the last presidents who wrote his own speeches. "He's also the only president with Native American blood, which interests people now," Cooke says. On the other hand, the organization Murder Victim Families for Reconciliation is inherently newsworthy because most people expect that the families of murder victims would be especially gung ho for the death penalty.

10. *Can you provide a pretext for a light, witty report?* Humor is always in demand. Dan Poynter, author of *The Self-Publishing Manual*, sent a tongue-in-cheek flyer to the media about what might otherwise have been just another seminar. After the headline, BOOT CAMP FOR PUBLISHERS, it ran for just eight sentences, beginning with, "If you've got the right stuff, Dan Poynter wants you for two days of training so rigorous you'll think you've joined the Marines! Join publishers from all over North America for this number one, high-intensity, combat marketing drill.... Class space is limited to the first eighteen recruits." *Publishers Weekly* and numerous other magazines picked up the story.

As you may have gathered, what lures the media may not be your central purpose or feature. If you have trouble figuring out what might interest masses of strangers about you or your business, ask a friend or colleague to help you answer that question. Fresh from her success in promoting *I Love Men in Tasseled Loafers*, Debbie Karpowicz helped her hairdresser get started in PR by getting him talking and learning that he used coffee to get rid of red highlights in hair. Karpowicz sent out sample packets of coffee stapled to a press release that started off, DISCOVER HOW TO PERK UP YOUR HAIR WITH COFFEE, and he received a call from *Allure* a week later. Her hairdresser wasn't running a coffee-treatment salon, but being mentioned in a national fashion magazine would stamp him as a somebody and lend him a valuable celebrity aura.

While timeliness is paramount, a few other factors can heighten the appeal of your story to the media. Will your story push the public's emotional buttons, either with tragedy or uplift? Editors and producers like to leaven death, doom, and destruction with classic crowd-pleasers like children, animals, and chocolate. Can you establish that your information impinges on huge numbers of people? If you've invented a device that helps people with bad backs, you've got better odds of wide press coverage than if your invention makes life easier for people who like to go snow camping. Or does your story resonate with some archetypal drama like "the big break" or "Joe Doe fights City Hall"? When retailer Rick Segel of Medford, Massachusetts, opened a men's clothing store, he twisted an advertising slogan made popular by a prominent competitor and got sued. "It was a 'David versus Goliath' story," he says, "irresistible to the media."

I'll get to the "hows" of approaching the media soon, but first I want to address the "yes, buts" that hold back many professionals, entrepreneurs, and people passionate about a cause from seeking the publicity that would benefit them.

CHAPTER 3

The Comfort Factor— Exposure Without Feeling Exposed

In the fall of 1980, I learned that the *New York Times* had decided to buy a personal essay I had written about the challenges and frustrations of college teaching. Before I had more than two minutes to celebrate, the telephone rang again. Someone from the *Times*'s photography department was on the line.

"We'd like to send out a photographer to take your picture," he said.

"You're kidding," I replied. So focused had I been on polishing the article to please the *Times* that this possibility hadn't occurred to me. It dampened my excitement. "Gee, I don't know if I want to have my picture in the *New York Times.*"

"Whyever not?"

I wasn't sure how to explain the reluctance I felt. "I don't know—it seems so, so publicity-seeking." I spat out those words.

The man chuckled. "No more than writing the article in the first place." He paused. "Come on, we'd like a photo. It'll be fine."

He did talk me into setting up a shoot with their photographer, but most of me felt relieved when the *Times* ended up running an illustration instead. Purely as an idea, the photo felt like some sort of encroachment on my view of myself. I knew this wasn't rational, but although I'd written a rather personal statement, so long as only my name appeared along with it, I felt I was putting it out into the world invisibly.

The details of my story are unique. I'll bet, though, that somewhere in your psyche lurk fears or discomforts about publicity—anywhere from one or two shadowy hangups to a whole truncheon-swinging gang of objections. Most people I've talked with, even those who appear to be born-with-a-horn self-promoters, get the creeps about at least some methods or circumstances of putting themselves forward. One friend told me that the first time she received a promotional flyer from me in the mail, her first thought was, "What chutzpah!" Cold calls or mailings to strangers didn't faze her, she explained, but she could never see herself sending something that talked herself up or asked for business from people she knew. A book author and consultant told me, "People who get to know me tell me I'm so smart, I should be charging more and have more of a public image. They're right, and I know that the problem goes all the way back to my childhood. It's my Achilles heel."

According to Brookline, Massachusetts, psychiatrist Michael Pearlman, resistances to promotion persist because of fears, unexamined beliefs, and deep confusions fostered by our culture, starting with the very term "self-promotion." "That's a contradiction in terms," he says. "You can't promote your *self*, only what's of value in what you do, which is an entirely separate thing from your self." Unconfronted fears about publicity may have wide-ranging ramifications for your ability to reach other goals, adds Joy Schmidt, who teaches entrepreneurial skills in Southfield, Michigan. "The very thing that keeps you from talking to the media may be holding back your business in general. The problem may be that you don't feel great about what you're doing. And in that case you can't pull customers in, because you're likely to be always thinking about yourself rather than the customer."

I hate seeing fears and misconceptions hold people back from receiving recognition that could be theirs. So I've designed this chapter to help you distinguish the concerns that are reasonable from those that have insinuated themselves into your head without good grounding. I'll also provide plenty of ammunition in case you decide to fight fears that seem to represent lost legacies from long ago. Whether your reluctance comes from constant admonitions not to show off while you were growing up, from viewpoints you absorbed when you were already grown, or from explicit thinking you've done about different ways to reach your goals, I'll show you how to find—and respect—your unique comfort zone with publicity. You *can* enjoy free media coverage without performing major surgery on your personality or forcing yourself to compromise your dignity.

Are Any of These Yours? Nineteen Prevalent Fears and Objections About Publicity

1. People Will Think I'm Bragging

If you shrink from marketing in general or feel a vague "ick" at the thought of media coverage, this one, deeply ingrained, might be the culprit. "Kids naturally get excited about what they can do, but lots of parents tell them, 'don't brag,'" says Nancy Michaels, owner of Impression Impact, a public relations firm in Concord, Massachusets. "So they learn not to talk about themselves. But seeking publicity isn't bragging. It's just letting people know what you do." When marketing consultant Tony Putman works with professionals who appear ambivalent about spreading the word about themselves, he gives them this definition: "Fundamentally, marketing in any form is helping people see what difference you're signing up to make in their life and the value and cost of what you have to offer to them. Through marketing, you enable potential customers to make the most accurate and appropriate decision they can make." He adds, "Unless someone has a deep issue with authority, it usually takes them only twenty to thirty minutes to get it."

The dialogue, I imagine, might go like this:

Q: Do you think there's value in what you do?
A: Of course. I'm an excellent doctor (lawyer, accountant, contractor). I save people's lives (safeguard their legal rights,

keep track of their finances, build fairly priced houses that last).

Q: Do you mind if people know how well you do that?

A: Of course not. I just don't think I should have to tell them.

Q: You just told me, though, and with total conviction.

A: Yes, but this wasn't for real. You weren't a reporter or a potential patient (client, customer).

Q: You mean to say you could be frank with me but not with the people in a position to have their lives saved (their rights or finances safeguarded, their housing needs satisfied), or with the people in a position to pass the word on to those people?

A: Uh ... (mental lightbulb goes on)

If you identify with this trepidation, you might try writing out your own dialogue like this, with one part played by the voice of reason, the other by the part of you that wants to appear selflessly absorbed in your work. Resolving the conflict isn't necessary for getting on with the business of publicity, however. If you feel it's too self-serving to tell or write the media about yourself, have someone else do it. Kenneth Palson of Worcester, Massachusetts, came in one day from feeding expired parking meters along Main Street in front of his hardware store and remarked to his brother Chuck, "Some day a reporter's going to come along and find out what I'm doing." Chuck Palson said, "How about today?" dialed the city desk of the *Worcester Telegram and Gazette*, and said, "You should have seen what I saw today on Main Street ..." Within hours, a reporter arrived to get the story. Like three other public relations professionals I spoke with, Nancy Michaels confessed that she has a hard time doing for herself what she does all the time for clients. She resolved the dilemma by deciding to start a newsletter directed toward her clients and putting the media on her subscription list. "That feels more comfortable for me than calling them up and talking about myself," she says.

2. I'd Feel Like I Was Begging

Linda Barbanel did have this thought when she graduated from her analytic training in 1980 and needed to lure patients into her office. But she quickly changed her attitude. "I'm not hustling, I'm helping people, and in order to help them they need to know that I'm available," she says. "I always present myself as a resource, and that way, I feel both professional and empowered." Another therapist, Szifra Birke, recalls having a newspaper reporter in one of her weekly groups. "She was always asking for story leads, and sometimes she was desperate for ideas. One day she pointed a finger in my face and said, 'The newspaper is a hungry animal, and it needs to be fed!' I've never forgotten that. It shocked me to think that they need us rather than the other way around." The media do need you, and if you approach them off your knees, you're more likely to precipitate an exchange that gratifies both parties.

3. People in My Field Don't Chase the Media— I'll Lose Respect and Credibility

Let me guess: You work in law, medicine, or academia. Until 1976 and 1979, respectively, the American Bar Association and the American Medical Association forbade members to advertise, and disapproval of blatant promotional efforts lingers in those professions. Stephen Kling, who works in health care advertising, used to specialize in helping doctors design promotional campaigns. "Doctors would tell me, 'Look, I'm sorry to be calling you,' and insist on meeting at night. It was as if they felt they were meeting a loan shark." Kling recalls cases where a doctor spent well into five figures and then pulled back, essentially throwing away the money, at the first whisper of criticism from colleagues. Academia never had written rules against advertising or promotion, but becoming a media star might conflict with the ivory-tower obscurity and footnotes-in-place correctness deemed appropriate for professors. Yet whatever your profession, you'll find options in this book that wouldn't reek of sleaze to even the fussiest of your colleagues. You can discreetly chase the media with no loss of self-respect or credibility.

4. You Have to Have a Lot of Nerve to Approach the Media

Have you ever called Mr. or Ms. Unapproachable for a date? Or dared to write a letter applying for a job you were sure thousands of other people wanted? Then you've got the right stuff to woo the press.

5. The Media Just Want Glitz, Sex, and Fluff

Yet the public is also hungry for inspiration and information, and the media often rise to the occasion of fulfilling those needs, too. "There are plenty of shows that are looking for content," says Paul Edwards, cohost of *Home Office*, which airs Sunday evenings on the non-glitz, non-fluff Business Radio Network. The media gladly spread the word about one of Joy Schmidt's clients, a children's clothing store that offers discounts to foster parents. Schmidt herself is blind and finds that practically anything she does makes an inspirational human interest story. "One reporter couldn't tear himself away from my talking computer," she laughs—again, no glitz, sex, or fluff.

6. If I Seek Out the Media, They'll Publicize My Competitors, Too

So what? If your competitors are honest players, you'll look good in their company. It might be time to update your attitude about competition. "I don't have competitors, just allies," says Jay Conrad Levinson, author of the "Guerrilla Marketing" books. "When people ask me if there's anyone else who does what I do, I mention Jeff Slutsky. We recommend each other and I don't have any problem with that at all. I fervently believe that we're in the age of cooperation, not competition." If Levinson's philosophy seems far out to you, just remember that if an article profiles you along with five other accountants, some readers may resonate with your comments and become clients. If other readers resonate with the comments of the other accountants, aren't you still better off than without the publicity?

7. I'll End Up Looking Like a Fool

Jeffrey Lant agrees with you here. "People are terrified of making a mistake," he says. "Don't worry—you will, and don't let that stop you." Lant recalls a lot of ridiculous situations he's landed in during his quest for publicity: radio stations that were broadcasting from closets, a TV host who interviewed him in a field, surrounded by cows. "Once I appeared on a show where the other guest was a woman who designed historical costumes for parrots. Just go with it," he advises. Early on Linda Barbanel swore during what she thought was a commercial break. To her mortification, the host informed her that they were on the air. The only consequence beyond the moment, though, was that it turned into a family joke. You'll make mistakes too. But is publicity-seeking really different in that respect from anything else you might do?

8. I'm Not a Born Publicity Hound, Like Donald Trump or Madonna

Bad examples! Unlike most of us, megamogul Donald Trump grew up with a role model in the house. When Donald was toddling around in his playpen, his father, real estate developer Fred Trump, used a public relations firm to issue press releases commenting on the state of the economy. But you can learn to exploit the media even if you come from a family that never went so far as to supply obituaries to the local paper. And as for rock star Madonna, at least one psychoanalyst has commented that she is addicted to provoking outrage. Rest assured that normal people can keep their publicity-seeking from spiraling to ever more shocking heights.

9. People Will Get Jealous of Me and Cut Me Down

Author/consultant Debra Benton recalls that when she began getting local publicity, people would say to her, "You're always in the newspaper," when she was written up just twice a year or so. This reminds me of a saying in China: "No pig wants to be the fattest; no tree wants to be the tallest in the forest." I'm not sure the thinnest pig or the shortest tree has a perfect life, either.

10. I'm Too Honest to Do Well with the Media

Have you been watching too many political debates? In fact, if you want to become a regular source for the media, you must be honest and avoid self-serving exaggerations, says Charlotte Ryan, author of *Prime Time Activism*. Provide reporters with relevant facts they don't have to double-check and you could be the environmentalist or missing-persons tracer they call to comment on breaking news.

11. Forget the Glory, I Want Proof That Time Spent on Publicity Will Show Up on the Bottom Line

You'll find publicity-seeking frustrating, says Stephen Kling, if you only feel comfortable in a world where spending ten dollars gets you ten dollars' worth of results and spending a thousand dollars gets you one hundred times those results. "You may get an avalanche of responses or nothing," says Paul Edwards. If you need indicators of what the possible avalanche might be worth to you, turn back to Chapter 1 and reread what happened with Trivial Pursuit and Jeff Slutsky.

12. My Services Are Confidential—I'll Lose Cachet from Publicity

Wisely or not, this didn't deter Harry Freedman, a stand-up comedian who is hired by corporations to fool their employees, from agreeing to a major feature and photo in the Sunday business section of the *New York Times*. Twice the article pointed out that if too many people knew he existed or what he looked like, his ability to pretend to be a top bank regulator or whatever could collapse. He replied that people have a habit of believing what they're told and that he looked like "a generic executive," so he wasn't worried. You may land in a more difficult bind if you guarantee confidentiality to those you serve and then can't provide the media with verifiable examples of what you've done. But don't worry about becoming uncool when you gain publicity. The prestige and payoff from being on the evening news more than outweigh being an in-group secret.

13. I'm Not the Sort of Person the Media Would Want to Promote

If you think you're not mediagenic, imagine someone who can't speak or walk and has only just enough movement in a few fingers to control his wheelchair and electronic voice synthesizer. That's Stephen Hawking, the theoretical physicist who wrote *A Brief History of Time*, has appeared in a *Vanity Fair* profile, and starred in a television documentary film about his life. As far as the media are concerned, the only flaw that disqualifies you from publicity is being boring—and even "The World's Most Boring Weatherman" could probably be made interesting on a slow news night.

14. How Can I Give Away My Secrets? That's How I Make My Living

One marketing consultant refused to speak to me for this book, giving this as a reason. My experience indicates that she was mistaken. After I published *Freelance Writing: Breaking in Without Selling Out*, I began giving seminars, thinking that people who attended a seminar would want to buy a book to take home. Many did, but to my surprise, people who had already bought the book showed up at the seminars too, plunking down up to eight times the cost of the book to hear in person what I had written. Grace Weinstein, who wrote *The Lifetime Book of Money Management* and has coordinated a conference on publicity and promotion for financial professionals, responds to this worry, "Readers may get some free advice when you're quoted but they'll never get enough to eliminate their need for professional help. Instead, they usually read what you said and say to themselves, 'Hey, this person knows something and might be able to help me solve my problem.'" So long as you have a depth of expertise, you'll find that media exposure increases rather than decreases the demand.

15. Too Much Publicity Would Be Bad— I Could Get Overexposed

No, the media spotlight doesn't do to people what too much sunlight does to film. Since 1977, when Joel Goodman created the Humor Project, an organization in Saratoga Springs, New York, that helps people focus on the positive power of humor and creativity in everyday life, he has appeared in the media more than 1,000 times, and says it only keeps on building and benefiting his cause. "We were the first organization in the world to do what we do, and we've generated more media on the subject than anyone else. Reporters tell me they saw my name in four out of five or five out of five of the articles they looked up, and that motivated them to call." When your reputation rests on a solid foundation, you remain the one to quote and invite on the air.

16. I'm Not Sure I Can Talk Coherently and Persuasively to the Media

Do you mean that you're not a natural talker? Then read Chapters 11, 14, 15, and 16 and practice. Or do you mean that you know how to do what you do but not explain it? Michael Pearlman, who co-leads workshops for entrepreneurs in addition to his psychiatric practice, told me that he doesn't feel ready to go to the *Boston Globe* about his program. Here I would say that if you're not ready, don't push it. Practice does help remedy this unreadiness, though, too. The more you talk about your offering to sympathetic friends, colleagues, and customers, the more confident you'll feel about being able to articulate its significance to the media.

17. I'll Lose My Privacy

I confess to this one. Recently I moved to a new community, picked up the local paper, and thought about sending them a press release and photo and getting coverage for my books and seminars. Then I reconsidered: Did I really want people recognizing me in the supermarket? Although I've had my picture on three book jackets, in several magazines, and in the *Boston Globe*, this remains almost as much of an issue for me as it was when I went through it with the *New York Times*. I continue to feel a tug between the safety of anonymity and the pleasure of acclaim. But I'm probably exaggerating the threat. Jay Conrad Levinson, who has many more books in print than I do and has had his full-page photo in *Entrepreneur*, says that people do recognize him, "but not much. I enjoy it because it's low-level and nonintrusive." Perhaps you have to be a politician, entertainer, athlete, or regular TV guest before you need protection from "Hey, you're ———, aren't you?"

18. It's So Manipulative

Yes, publicity-seeking often involves calculated moves, but that doesn't necessarily make it deceptive, corrupt, or unscrupulous. On the contrary, most of those I spoke with who consistently get media coverage said that without wholespirited enthusiasm, they wouldn't have been able to win over reporters and producers. Sheer manipulativeness, in other words, doesn't work. "You have to be excited *and* have some real substance to offer," says Ron Bianco, who has successfully courted the media through phone calls and letters. Saying that he has a singing dog usually gets him attention, but, he adds, "It's also always important that I have a bona fide show."

19. I Don't Know How to Do It

Aha, that's the easiest of them all for me to respond to. Just read the remainder of this book!

I may have missed your particular qualms, so to complete your self-assessment, you may want to take a few minutes for the following exercise. It's simple enough that you should be able to read it and remember it without having to reread or tape-record the directions. Close your eyes and let yourself become deeply relaxed. Then imagine yourself having achieved flattering national publicity. Notice what that looks like, sounds like, and feels like. Also notice all the consequences of publicity, and what they look like, sound like, and feel like. All in all, is this what you want? Notice a signal that means "yes," "maybe," or "no."

Exploring Your Comfort Zone

Let's say that you identified with several of the concerns listed above. Now what? The next step is to find the ways of seeking publicity that feel comfortable for you. Observe your reactions as you read or reread the dozens of examples sprinkled throughout this book. Which of the things that others have done can you see yourself doing too? Which get you talking to yourself, walking around the house restlessly, or jotting down plans on scrap paper? Which provoke a warm, surprised feeling of inspiration? All these constitute clues to publicity methods that you can wholeheartedly commit yourself to. Also take note of the possibilities that attract you but also somewhat scare you. Those probably lie at the border of your comfort zone. With a little imaginative reflection, you can include those in your repertoire, too. In my studies of creativity and procrastination, I've found that people have idiosyncratic, personal patterns of what enables them to painlessly accomplish something new. Use these questions to tune into *your* tendencies.

1. *Do you like to plunge right into new things or wade in gradually?* If someone at the pool tells you the water's cold and you characteristically go ahead and dive in anyway, then you might want to start out with your first publicity blitz to the major media. That won't feel right to you, though, if you prefer to walk in up to your knees, splash water onto your arms and chest, and go ahead only when you feel acclimated. In that case, start out with local media or on professionally familiar territory, venturing further when you get used to the process.

2. *Are you more comfortable with speaking or with writing?* If you're naturally eloquent and persuasive when you talk and hate trying to get the same effect on paper, then take everything I say in Chapter 4 under advisement and concentrate on phone pitches and schmoozing instead. If, however, you start to stammer whenever you're on the spot, put your effort into written materials that are so terrific that they practically eliminate the need for followup interviews.

3. *Do you believe that modesty is next to godliness or have you been your own best promoter since you ran for sixth-grade president?* If you've always flinched at being asked to sell yourself at job interviews, no one says you have to shine the spotlight on yourself. Put and keep the spotlight on your product, your service, or your customers. Think of yourself as the stagehand, who pads around in black backstage to keep the set arranged. But if you love being under klieg lights, you've probably already invented creative publicity tactics of your own, and I'd love to hear about them.

4. *Would you rather lurk behind the scenes or sit in the glory seat out front?* During the existence of WordRight, I wrote most of our press releases and my partner talked to the reporters who called. Although that meant that her name got into the papers more than mine, I didn't care. I'd already seen my name in print a lot, and she got more of a kick out of gabbing with reporters than I did. You can always designate, and train, a contact person to speak for your organization if you find interviews bothersome. Your son or daughter, your summer intern, or your receptionist might have the enthusiasm that would make a great spokesperson.

5. *How concerned are you about the tackiness factor?* Although some people with a substantial media presence appear to have sought the limelight, others come off as if acclaim and attention were thrust on them. You can seek publicity *and* maintain a dignified professional image by choosing your tactics carefully. Instead of firing out indiscriminate inquiries, contact a science reporter for the *Los Angeles Times* or someone else whose work you respect. Persuade an ambitious former student to develop an intellectually informed piece for the *Atlantic Monthly.* Write letters to the editor that correct mistakes in your area of expertise. Prepare fact sheets that remain true to the complexity of your views.

6. *Are you a loner or someone who always gravitates to groups?* Although I've addressed you throughout this book as if you were seeking publicity alone, if that doesn't appeal to you, why not form a Publicity Team or Publicity Club so that you can cheer and coach each other through the process? Or designate someone as your Publicity Buddy and keep each other on track. Critique one another's press releases over lunch, lick stamps together, and celebrate each other's triumphs.

7. *Do you do best when the stakes are high or when it doesn't matter if you fail?* I've heard people say, "I *had* to go all out. I'd have lost my house to the bank otherwise." If high stakes motivate you, plunk down a nonrefundable fee for a giant auditorium and then get busy generating the publicity that will sell out the hall. If the mere thought of losing it all paralyzes you with fear, tie your first publicity push to an event that will come off well without any press at all.

Overall, maximize what you enjoy and minimize what you dread. And, to adapt a saying of George Orwell, ignore any advice in this book sooner than violate your educated sense of what's right for you. In other words, after reading and thinking about my suggestions, if you find yourself thinking, "I really ought to . . . but it gives me a headache," don't. Either modify my advice or hunt back through the book for an alternative that sits as well with you as a perfect-fitting pair of pants.

WRITING
TO GET
PUBLICITY

CHAPTER 4

Six Steps to Free Publicity—The Easiest, Fastest, Cheapest Way to Get Featured in the Media

Up till now I've avoided using the term "press release" so that I could orient you and help you get comfortable and focused with publicity. But now it's time to introduce you to the basic tool for gaining the attention of the media.

A press release is a brief document in a specific format that demonstrates to newspeople why you or your business merit media coverage now. It usually takes up just one page, at most two, and doesn't require fancy typesetting or design. Hence it fits any budget. Its power lies in its compact, scannable format and in the compelling way in which you answer that all-important question dissected in Chapter 2: Why would our readers/listeners/viewers be interested in this story now?

Before I take you step by step through the process of writing your own release, I'd like you to take a look at one example of this miracle-working species of correspondence. Upon receiving the following press release, which I produced for a client, several boat magazine editors called immediately to say they would be featuring Gabison's product in an upcoming issue.

For: Tarpaulin Drainage Systems, 14553 SW 77 St.,
  Miami, FL 33183.
Contact: Daniel Gabison, (305) 256-0075.

FOR IMMEDIATE RELEASE

NEW DRAINAGE SYSTEM SAVES BOAT OWNERS TOIL AND EXPENSE

Miami, February 11, 1993—Among those who dread rain most are boat owners. Until now, every one of them watching a downpour has known either that they'll have to get over to their boat soon and bail out the buckets of water accumulating on their boat cover or, although they've installed a system to drain the water, it is endangering the longevity of their tarpaulin. Now, however, boat owners can buy peace of mind with a simple Punch-Drain that removes rainwater automatically, protecting the boat and prolonging the life of their boat cover.

"The Punch-Drain came to me out of necessity," says Miami-based boat owner Daniel Gabison, the inventor. "In the rainy season, my boat cover would fill with water, and I'm not talking about just a bucket or two. Although I drained the water every few days, after a short time the tarpaulin would start to sag, tear and deteriorate under the great weight of the collected water."

Gabison tried the two available systems designed to prevent water from accumulating, both of which required the tarpaulin to be stretched tight, so that the device either itself broke or tore a hole in the tarpaulin. Instead of trying to keep the tarpaulin tight, Gabison designed a solution that got rid of the water while leaving the tarpaulin slack. His Punch-Drain, patented in 1991, drains rainwater straight to the bilge, from which it drains out through the boat's bilge hole.

The Punch-Drain, all American made, costs just $14.95 and is available through boat supply stores or direct from Tarpaulin Drainage Systems, 14553 SW 77 St., Miami, FL 33183. For more information, boat owners or dealers can call (305) 256-0075.

Can you see how obvious it is on even a quick read how boat owners would benefit from learning about Gabison's invention?

Now here's how to produce an effective press release of your own.

Six Steps to Free Publicity

Step One: Find a News Angle for Your Headline

Select one or more of these ten media hooks, discussed in more detail in Chapter 2.

- Something new about your business or organization
- What's distinctive about you or your business
- An upcoming event
- Connection between what you offer and current news
- Survey or poll research
- A contest or award
- Tie-in with a holiday or anniversary
- Connection between what you offer and a current trend
- Controversial or surprising claim
- Humorous announcement

Then compose an eye-catching, informative headline using that hook. The headline can take up more than one line on the release, so go on as long as necessary to complete the idea. If possible, include the benefit to media audiences in the headline. Just as in newspaper headlines, you can use a compressed, telegraphic style. For example:

- OLYMPIC COACH RECOMMENDS ANAEROBICS—NO-SWEAT EXERCISE—FOR COUCH POTATOES
- FEBRUARY 17 EXECUTIVE PANEL TO PROFFER STRATEGIES FOR SUCCESS IN A STAGNANT ECONOMY
- DURANGO'S ONLY THEME PARK OPENS CHILD-CARE CENTER

Step Two: Present the Basic Facts for the Angle of Your Headline in Paragraph One

Answer the journalist's "Five W's": Who? What? When? Where? Why (or how)? Notice that I said "the basic facts *for the angle of your headline*," not the basic facts about your product or service or you. In many cases, these are not the same. For instance, in the first paragraph of the press release above, I didn't include the who, what, when, where, and why about the invention of the Punch-Drain, but about how it saves boat owners toil and expense, the angle stated in the headline.

Who: Boat owners

What: They can buy a device called the Punch-Drain that removes rainwater automatically from boat tarpaulins

When: Now

Where: Implicitly, anywhere boats get rained on

Why: To protect their boat and prolong the life of the boat cover

Weave your who, what, when, where, and why together in an opening paragraph for your release. If you can make your pitch catchy, fine. But a straightforward, factual style does the job, too.

Step Three: Gather or Create a Lively Quote That Elaborates on the Basic Facts for Paragraph Two

Here you quote someone who can back up the basic claim of the release—you; the company president; the originator of the event, product, or service; a satisfied customer; or someone who carries special weight with your target audience. A quote enables you to bring the story to life, provide perspective, or add star appeal. For example, in a release I wrote for a conference linking large New England companies and potential small-business suppliers, I quoted Massachusetts senator John Kerry on why he had signed on as a sponsor of the conference. Chapter 19 tells you how to get useful quotes from others to use in publicity, but often you really will be the optimum person to quote, and you can have fun here putting words into your own mouth.

Step Four: Elaborate Further on the Basic Facts in Paragraph Three

What else do you want to communicate to editors and producers? You can continue to quote yourself, quote someone besides whoever you quoted in paragraph two, or report additional facts that support your claims in straight prose. You might want to place biographical information about you or historical data about your subject here. I didn't include much about Daniel Gabison because he wasn't an expert in boat design and his regular job had nothing to do with being a boat owner who had invented a better drainage solution that would help others like him. Don't distract, support your story!

Step Five: End with the Nitty-Gritty Details

What are the practical details (prices, addresses, dates, phone numbers, how to register, etc.) that any media notice about your subject should include? Combine these details in a sentence or two. At this point you'll have drafted a four-paragraph press release. Congratulations! Polish it and print it up in the format of this and the previous example.

For: WordRight, Suite 123, 20 Main St.,
  Boston, MA 00000.
Contact: Marcia Yudkin, (617) 555-5555.

FOR IMMEDIATE RELEASE

LOCAL COMMUNICATION CONSULTANTS
PUBLISH *SMART SPEAKING*

Boston, MA, April 1, 1991—On April 19, Henry Holt is publishing *Smart Speaking: Sixty Second Strategies* by local communication experts Laurie Schloff and Marcia Yudkin. Schloff, a senior consultant at The Speech Improvement Company in Brookline, and Yudkin, Vice-President of WordRight in Boston, teamed up to write this easy-reference, fast-paced guide to overcoming more than 100 common speaking problems and fears. Excerpts appear in the April issue of *Ladies Home Journal* and the May issue of *Cosmopolitan*.

"An indispensable book that can aid anyone in getting ahead," says Applied Management Systems President Alan Goldberg of *Smart Speaking*. The book offers solutions for communication problems from accents to breathiness, cold calls to small talk, pressured presentations to unproductive meetings, and forgetting names to gaucheness at a business lunch.

Laurie Schloff, a resident of Newton, based the tips in *Smart Speaking* on her decade of experience coaching private clients and executives and employees at organizations like Polaroid, Harvard University, Massachusetts General Hospital and the Ritz Carlton. A founder of the Fear of Speaking Association, Schloff has also taught at Northeastern University.

Marcia Yudkin, who lives in Boston's South End, brought her experience writing three previous books and articles for publications like *Ms., Psychology Today,* the *Boston Globe* and the *New York Times* to *Smart Speaking*. For the last three years she has offered seminars on becoming a more productive and effective writer and helped individuals polish their writing to professional standards.

"Ironically, I became more interested in writing while working on the book," says Schloff, who has been speaking in public since the age of four, "while Marcia, the writer, became more interested in speaking." Based on the preliminary response to their book, including the sale of rights to the Newbridge Book Club and nine companies bidding for paperback rights, the two communication consultants are already planning a sequel to *Smart Speaking.*

Schloff and Yudkin both offer workshops at the Boston Center for Adult Education and, through The Speech Improvement Company and WordRight, to businesses nationwide.

I wrote the above release because our publisher had sent a review package for our book to our city's two major newspapers, the *Globe* and the *Herald,* and we wanted to assure coverage in the smaller papers that hit our neighborhood or town as well. We also wanted to tie our consulting practices to the book. It worked! I received a front-page profile and photo in the *South End News,* while my coauthor landed in the pages of several papers that serve Newton, where she lives, and Brookline, where she works. Here, as in the previous sample, using the standard press release format gives editors all the information they need exactly where they're accustomed to getting it.

First line: Provide your business name and address on the top line.

Second line: Supply a name and number editors can call for more information. Make sure that the contact person can speak knowledgeably and in detail about the subject of the press release. If you want to look like you have a bigger operation than you do, and come off as if you're not blowing your own horn, make up a nonexistent person whose name you always use on press releases. Then, when a call comes in for, say, "Trudy Einhorn," you know it's from the media and you can say, "Trudy's not here at the moment. This is Joe Business. May I help you?"

"For Immediate Release": This signals that editors can use the story immediately. If you've run a contest and don't want the winners' names released until May 15, 1994, you'd write instead, "For Release May 15, 1994."

Headline: Capitalize, center and underline this, and if possible, use boldface and slightly larger type. Running to three lines for the headline is perfectly okay.

Dateline: Write the city, state, and date for the story's origin. This imparts a nice journalistic flavor. Plan carefully so that you mail your copies of a release on or a bit later than the date stated here.

Format: Indent paragraphs, double-space the release, and use the informal look of ragged right margins rather than justified (straight-down-the-page) right margins. Keep it to one page if possible. I printed out the *Smart Speaking* release in a compressed typeface that enabled me to fit the whole text on one page. If you must continue to a second sheet, write "(more)" on the bottom of page one and your business name and "(continued)" at the top of page two. Many editors say they prefer plain white paper to company letterheads, which may also leave you less space for text than plain paper. Margins of an inch or more on all sides leave enough space for your recipient to scribble editing notes.

Step Six: Send It Out

You don't need any sort of cover letter, but it helps a lot to address releases to a specific editor or producer by name. Since the necessary media directories tend to cost several hundred dollars each, I recommend you use the reference sources at your local library, such as:

Bacon's Newspaper/Magazine Directory (directory of newspapers and magazines)

Bacon's Radio/TV/Cable Directory (directory of radio, TV, and cable stations and shows)

Standard Periodical Directory (directory of magazines)

Gale Directory of Publications and Broadcast Media (directory of newspapers, magazines, radio and TV stations)

Editor and Publisher International Yearbo
newspapers)

Working Press of the Nation (directory i
radio/TV; magazines and in-house publicatic
freelance photographers and writers)

Newsletters in Print (largest directory of newsletters)

Oxbridge Directory of Newsletters (directory of newsletters)

Encyclopedia of Associations (directory of professional,
trade, and cultural organizations, many of which publish
newsletters or magazines)

Standard Rate and Data Service (directory of magazines in
two volumes: business publications; consumer publications)

All of the above are profiled in more detail in Chapter 23.
Also, ask your librarian about a reference guide to your local
media. For California you'll find *Metro California Media*, for the
New York City area, *New York Publicity Outlets*, and so on. For
TV and radio shows, remember to address your release to the
producer, not the host.

Getting the press releases addressed, stamped, and mailed is
definitely the most tedious part of the whole process. Consider
hiring a high school student with good handwriting to address
envelopes for you from the directories in the library. Or borrow
a portable computer and enter the data from the reference
books, which you'd have to do only once. In Chapter 23 I've
listed a few inexpensive sources for media lists on disk and in
print.

Additional Tips for Getting the Greatest Mileage from Your Press Releases

1. *Keep the tone objective, not promotional.* Hype, unsubstan-
tiated superlatives, or direct sales pitches ("VimVy Vitamins will
make you stronger, sexier, and sassier") all kill interest in giving
you free media space or time. Whenever you want to include an
opinion or praise, attribute it to someone—a real person only!—

stick it within quotes. " 'VimVy Vitamins will make you stronger, sexier, and sassier,' says Hypatia Hiram, a customer since 1988," is more likely to survive screening.

2. *Proofread rigorously.* Editors have told me that if they spot a single typo or misspelling in a release, they toss it out. Send your release through the checklist in Chapter 17 to eliminate other common writing errors. Don't depend on your spell-check program; even the smartest ones miss some dumb mistakes.

3. *Produce different versions of your release for separate, distinct audiences.* When Dan Poynter was issuing a new edition of his *The Parachute Manual*, he sent out three releases, one for each market his book appealed to. For piloting and aviation magazines, he used the headline, SKYDIVING = A NEW WAY TO FLY, for sports magazines he talked about parachuting as the fastest nonmechanical sport, and for parachutists, most of whom were probably already familiar with his book, he made a straightforward announcement that a new edition was available. "In talking about skydiving as a way to fly, I was using language that pilots could relate to, but experienced skydivers would think that was dumb," says Poynter. Similarly, in connection with this book I have prepared releases for legal magazines and tabloids that start off, NEW BOOK HELPS LAWYERS OVERCOME FEAR OF PROMOTION, releases for dental magazines that begin, NEW BOOK HELPS DENTISTS OVERCOME FEAR OF PROMOTION, and so on.

4. *Plan to be available after you distribute your release.* Just before you head off to Europe for three weeks is not a good time to send off press releases. Chapters 14 and 22 reveal other ways to get and keep journalists on your side. For daily newspapers, radio, or TV, send your stuff out at least two weeks before any date on which you'd like coverage; for weekly papers, a month ahead. For monthly magazines, three or four months ahead is wise. Allow even longer lead times for bimonthly or quarterly periodicals.

If you've written a decent press release that appears complete, some media outlets will run it word for word, condense it, or rewrite it, embellishing on the information you sent them. Others will call you up to get additional information, satisfy themselves that you are legitimate, or invite you to be a guest on their program. If you hear only a loud, resounding silence, this does not mean you've done anything wrong. Make sure you've followed all my guidelines and try again. Even Madonna's redoubtable press agent can't get her exposure everywhere, all the time.

There's one variant on the formulas above that I'd like to share with you before we turn to supporting materials for your press releases. Particularly for magazines, sometimes you'll want to issue a press release that isn't timely but does offer useful, well-targeted information for a certain audience. In the following release for writing publications, you'll notice that I omitted the dateline and didn't really meet any of my ten tests for timeliness. Nevertheless, because the content was fresh, interesting, and beneficial to writers, a good number of the newsletters I targeted used it. If you're hoping to spread the word about your expertise, I'd recommend releasing a series of tips like this on a regular basis.

For: Creative Ways, P.O. Box 1310,
   Boston, MA 02117.
Contact: Marcia Yudkin, (617) 266-1613.

FOR IMMEDIATE RELEASE

STANDING DESKS AND UNSTICKING LETTERS: HOW TO FIND YOUR MAGICALLY IDIOSYNCRATIC WRITING METHOD

Boston, MA—Have you ever tried writing standing up? Ernest Hemingway, Virginia Woolf and Lewis Carroll wrote their masterpieces at standing desks. When you're stuck, have you tried writing a letter about what you would say if you could write your piece? That's how Tom Wolfe invented the "New Journalism." Writer and writing consultant Marcia Yudkin, Ph.D., suggests ways for writers to find their uniquely comfortable, procrastination-beating ways to write.

1. *Claim your strengths.* Complete this sentence, which appears to conjure up your weaknesses: "I can only write when . . ." Then use the answers as clues to the conditions that do get you writing. If you can only write at the office, then go in early

to work on your novel; if only deadlines get you moving, ask friends to create them for you.

2. *Consider and use what motivates you outside of writing.* A consultant who wanted to write fiction realized that she enjoyed doing things for others rather than herself; she started and finished her first short story as a gift for her goddaughter. An artist turned playwright sketched his characters, drew symbolic illustrations of his themes and visited art museums when he needed inspiration on new plot turns.

3. *Pay attention to subtle sensory signals.* Erica Jong says she knows a poem is coming on when the hair on the back of her neck stands up. John Fowles created *The French Lieutenant's Woman* out of a dream image. Other authors hear their muse whispering words to them. Some quiet time every day will help you learn to recognize these faint but precious hints from your unconscious.

4. *Try ways to write that sound bizarre.* Friedrich Schiller wrote best when he kept rotten apples in his desk. Carolyn Chute acts out all her characters' parts as she writes. Natalie Goldberg makes appointments with her friends to meet at a café, write for an hour, talk and drink tea, then write more. Rent a tiger suit or go out on the roof to write; you wouldn't be the first to laugh yourself onto the bestseller list.

Marcia Yudkin is the author of five books, including *Freelance Writing*, offered by the Book-of-the-Month Club. She has produced three audiotapes that help listeners write with more ease: *Exploding Writer's Block, Become a More Productive Writer,* and *Procrastination: Creative Solutions.* To receive a copy of her booklet, "77 Ways for Writers to Get Unstuck," send $1.00 and a self-addressed stamped envelope to her at P.O. Box 1310, Back Bay Station, Boston, MA 02117.

Although Chapter 16 discusses a way to get the attention of key media people without spending a cent on copying or postage, I still consider press releases the easiest, most cost-effective method. You never know in advance which media outlets will respond with interest, and by mailing press releases, you can reach dozens or hundreds simultaneously. Many public relations professionals insist that you must call recipients of your press releases to follow up. But most of the individuals I spoke with for this book whose businesses get constant press never—never—make follow-up calls. Hence I'd say that although polite follow-up calls along the lines of "Did you receive my press release?" may sometimes provide an extra-opportunity nudge, they're not necessary. Just write your most compelling, carefully targeted press release and, in Dan Poynter's words, "Lick it, stick it, and drop it in the mail." Then watch the results pile up.

CHAPTER 5

Supporting the Story with a Press Kit

Most of you, I'm assuming, don't have large publicity budgets at your disposal. Hence the common request, "Please send me your press kit," might provide you cause for alarm. It sounds fancy and intimidating, doesn't it? Yet a press kit is nothing more than a packet of materials that you send any member of the media when he or she asks for it, or that you send in advance when you are trying to appear on a major talk show. Its contents reinforce your claim to be worthy of publicity. Except for the photographs, you can prepare everything that you need to back up your story for the media by visiting any office supply store and a copy shop.

Components of a Press Kit

Of the following ingredients, those preceded by a star are standard and pretty much required; those preceded by a dash are optional.

*A Black-and-White Glossy Photo, either 5" by 7" or 8" by 10"

Caption it on the back with your name and contact information. Instead of writing on the back of the photo with a pen, use a sticker or mailing label printed with the information or write with a felt tip marker. Generally the media prefer a head shot. Most professional photo labs offer bulk rates for twelve or more copies of the same shot. If you think you'll need hundreds of photos, you can save hundreds of dollars by ordering lithographs instead. They look fine to the uneducated eye and their quality is clear enough for publication in newspapers and most magazines. See Chapter 23 for a wholesale source of publicity lithographs.

Your photo should fit the image you want to project without looking clichéd. According to Nat Starr of Troy, Michigan, who specializes in advertising for professional speakers, overdone poses include holding a trophy, posing on a platform with your mouth open as if you're talking, shaking hands with someone else, pretending to write or talk on the phone, and pointing at something, like your product. To that list I would add, for highbrow types, the "Thinker" pose (chin resting on knuckles). Jeff Davidson, author of *Blow Your Own Horn* and seventeen other books, updates his photos often and keeps different pictures on hand. "It's boring," he says, "to see the same picture of someone used over and over for years."

*A Bio (Biography) of You or Your Business or Both, in Paragraph Form

Do not enclose a résumé. You are not applying for a job! The bio should highlight your most important accomplishments, particularly recent ones, and should make you sound interesting. For a press kit you'll need a one-page biographical description about yourself or your organization—both if the organization has a significantly different history from your own. A press release will usually contain a condensed, one-paragraph version of your bio, as will your own marketing materials. A one-sentence version comes in handy as a blurb to accompany articles by you or in "coming attractions" notices about you.

Whatever the size or slant of the bio, begin with a catchy summary first sentence. Lead off with the most important thing or things you want the reader to know about you or the business. For example:

"Helen Planetstein has been active in the save-the-whales movement since 1979, when she helped publicize the plight of a beached whale on Cape Cod."

"A certified plumber and electrician for the past fifteen years, Tom Reilly launched his inventing career in 1988 with a patented, nontoxic drain declogger."

"Quintabulousness, Inc., an interior design firm for hardened individualists, is the creation of local socialite Beverly Monoppilino."

Then add supporting details in the following sentences.

You needn't arrange facts in strict chronological order. It's usually better to go in order of decreasing importance. Remember that the purpose of the bio is to present background information in an engaging way, not to be comprehensive. Accordingly, you need to select ruthlessly what needs to be included and what can be left out. Customarily, bios use third person (he/she/it/they) rather than first person (I). When you edit and polish your bio, think lively and think specific. Use complete sentences and paragraphs, instead of the clipped style typical of résumés; make sure your final version passes all the tests in Chapter 17.

Following are the dual bios I wrote in 1990 to accompany the book *Smart Speaking*, by Laurie Schloff and myself, and then the condensed bios that appeared on the book jacket. In the longer version I avoided the dry, flat tone of the average bio.

Full-Length Version of Bios

Laurie Schloff's speaking career began at the age of four when she sang 14 verses of "Davy Crockett" to 200 folks at a nursing home in Old Orchard Beach, Maine. She officially entered the field of speech with a master of science degree in speech pathology from Columbia University and a certificate of clinical competence from the American Speech-Language-Hearing Association. Since 1980 Laurie has been a senior communication consultant with The Speech Improvement Company, a nationwide communication consulting firm based in the Boston area. She works with clients in all walks of life, from attorneys to zoologists, and from secretaries to executives at companies that include Polaroid, John Hancock Insurance, Hit or Miss, the Ritz Carlton Hotel, Digital Equipment Corporation, AT&T, Massachusetts General Hospital and Harvard University.

Although Marcia Yudkin played the Cowardly Lion in *The Wizard of Oz* at summer camp at age 12, she didn't become serious about public appearances until going on the lecture circuit after the 1988 publication of her third book, *Freelance Writing for Magazines and Newspapers*. She has been a keynote speaker at numerous writers' conferences and presents workshops on creativity and getting published coast to coast. Marcia has a doctorate in philosophy from Cornell University and is Vice-President of WordRight, which provides writing seminars and consulting services to companies and individuals in Boston and throughout the Northeast.

Condensed Version of Bios

Laurie Schloff is a senior consultant with The Speech Improvement Company in Boston. She has taught at the university level, consulted with major corporations and conducts workshops nationwide. Marcia Yudkin is a founder of WordRight, a Boston writing consulting company, and the author of *Freelance Writing for Magazines and Newspapers*.

—Articles by or About You

These should be readably photocopied, with some indication of where and when the pieces appeared. Many people clip the masthead or logo of the publication (i.e., the name of the publication in its distinctive type style) and paste it up together with the article. This can catch attention better than simply writing the publication's information in the margin by hand.

—Tip Sheets by You

These are lists like "Ten Ways to Mouseproof Your Cellar" or "Seven Reasons You're Probably Paying More Taxes Than You Should" that are equivalent to articles but haven't been published. See Chapter 7 for more on why and how to put these together. If you can't do desktop publishing yourself, take them to a place that can format and typeset them nicely for you.

—Press Releases

Include any that are relatively recent and that still characterize you or your business.

—Other Marketing or Publicity Material

If you have a brochure, include it.

—Media Contact Sheet

If you've been featured in the press or on radio or TV several times before, include a list of the publications or shows.

—Quote Sheet

If you have three or more testimonials from authoritative figures or from media reviews, print them up together as in the following sample, concerning Sandra Weintraub's "Harasser Flasher" pin. Include attribution for all quotes, or they are meaningless. See Chapter 19 on how to obtain and edit testimonials.

Sample Quote Sheet

Management Resources

What Others Are Saying About the Harasser Flasher . . .

"Men often do not hear a woman's voice when that voice seeks to set boundaries. The Harasser Flasher will punctuate a woman's intentions and expectations to what is off limits in that relationship . . . and it should be particularly useful on college campuses and in party settings."

Francine Solomon, Ph.D., psychologist

"In one study, 76 percent of harassed women used the strategy of ignoring the harasser to try to get the offensive behavior to stop. Frequently, however, that didn't work. The Harasser Flasher pin will give women one more communication tool, increasing the odds of the message getting through."

Marcia Yudkin, Ph.D., co-author, *He & She Talk: Communicating with the Opposite Sex* (Plume)

"I think that the Harasser Flasher pin will accomplish several goals: It will allow women to warn men of improper sexual advances without having to go through embarrassing verbal jousts; it will make men aware of their unconscious sexual attitudes that are culturally defined and derogatory towards women; and it will help raise the male consciousness in the work place. A superhuman task in itself!"

Arthur Bernard, Ph.D., Director of the Dream Center, Sherman Oaks, CA, and author, teacher, psychologist

"The question again, is what do women want. This time, I think I've found the answer. It's a nifty . . . little technological advance that will fundamentally and forever alter the relationship between men and women. Not only that, it (the Harasser Flasher) accessorizes."

Mike Littwin, Syndicated Columnist, *Baltimore Sun*

"The Harasser Flasher is costume jewelry for these troubled and confusing times, a pin designed to warn sexual harassers that they are treading on thin ice."

Diane White, Syndicated Columnist, *Boston Globe*

"Percentage of men who think women give mixed signals: 72. For men totally confused about sexual harassment in the workplace, there's now a device to help them read the signals. . . . When a man makes an unwarranted sexual comment, women use the gadget to flash a red light."

Eyewitness, *Details Magazine*, February 1993

—Fact Sheet

Whenever you can provide an easy-reference roster of facts about your subject, you position yourself as a credible information source. Since fact sheets are likely to be saved and quoted from in issue-oriented articles that do not focus on your business, print yours on a letterhead or include all your contact information so you'll receive credit if they're separated from your press kit.

Sample Fact Sheet

Working From **Home**

Newsletters, Directories and Seminars for Independent Consultants, Entrepreneurs and Small Business

The Working From Home Profile

- The homeworker population is comprised of three groups. The first is those whose primary income is from at-home self-employment. The second group is made up of those who hold a full-time job, but run a part-time business from their home to supplement their income. The third group is telecommuters. These are company employees working from home and connected to head office through computers and faxes.

- Helping fuel today's trend are powerful tools like fax machines, cellular telephones, voice mail, cost-effective 1-800 toll-free phone numbers, computerized information services and personal computers that have dropped dramatically in price. The flourishing low-cost courier business has also had a positive impact.

- These tools allow the homeworker to produce professional results without the need for a large support staff.

- Other reasons fueling this trend are minimal capital required for startup, low ongoing overhead, unlimited income potential, a flexible work schedule (important for quality family time), self-employed tax benefits, and independence.

- Some interesting information on the homeworker
  - their average age is 41
  - 61 percent are male
  - 39 percent are female
  - 77 percent are married

- 64 percent have children
- average number of children is two
- 38 percent run a full-time home-based business
- 30 percent run a part-time home-based business

- The top three reasons they decided to start their own business:
    1. Wanted to be their own boss
    2. Wanted less routine in their life
    3. Wanted to change their life

- The top three businesses:
    1. Business consulting and services
    2. Computer services/programming
    3. Financial consulting and services

- Who is working from home? The list is almost limitless and includes consultants, writers, accountants, photographers, graphic designers, architects, salespeople, insurance agents, bookkeepers, public relations specialists, computer programmers/analysts, real estate agents, contractors, meeting planners, secretarial services, interior designers, artists, professional speakers, property managers, translators, trade show organizers, entrepreneurs, and small business.

For more information call toll free 1-800-283-3008 in the U.S.A. and Canada.

P.O. Box 1722, Hallandale, Florida 33008 • Phone 1-800-283-3008: U.S.A. and Canada

---

IDEAS THAT WORK FOR YOU TODAY!

—Talking Points

If you're aiming for radio or TV, you can include a list of questions the host can ask. These should be intriguing questions designed to lead into what you want to talk about, such as, "What do you think is the biggest mistake most entrepreneurs make?" or "You've said that there are three situations in which people can do their own divorce. What are they?" The purpose is not to show journalists how to do their job but to get them interested in finding out the answers from you—on the air. Alternatively, you can provide a crisp, concise list of your major points if you think your answers will be more compelling than the questions.

—Client List

Consultants or seminar leaders who do business with famous corporations, organizations, or individuals may want simply to enumerate them, without any quotes. If your list begins, "AT&T; Bell Labs; CalTech Alumni Association; Data General . . ." that's almost as strong as fantastic quotes.

—Photo or Sample of Product

Some inventors or manufacturers will want to enclose a sample of what they make or information on how to get it. Jim Scott, maker of Great Scott! fudge, says that a scrumptious sample of his product along with a press release helped win him features in *Bon Appetit, Food & Wine, Chocolatier,* and the *Los Angeles Times*.

Generally people place these materials in a 9" by 12" colored folder with pockets. Linda Barbanel makes a subtle statement with folders in green—the color of money, her theme. She hasn't found any other sort of customization necessary. But if you like, you can personalize generic folders by pasting your business card neatly on the front. Book authors can paste extra book covers, or a color copy of the book jacket, on the front of the folders. Whenever possible, include your contact information on each item in the packet, since recipients may separate parts of the kit.

Creative Press Kits

If your service or product lends itself to humor or fantasy, sure, get creative. But try something cute to promote your blue-chip investment brokerage, and you'll usually just be laughed right into the wastebasket. Debbi Karpowicz did get an excellent response when she sent out press kits for her book, *I Love Men in Tasseled Loafers*, in bona fide shoe boxes. Each contained a press release rolled up and tied with a leather loafer tassel that she had persuaded the Allen-Edmonds shoe company to donate. The photo that was enclosed showed her in a nearly backless gown, looking seductively over her shoulder while holding up a man's loafer. Just as appropriately, actor Norman George's promotional photo shows him dressed in period costume as Edgar Allan Poe, the focus of his show *Poe Alone*. George encloses a twelve-inch black feather reminiscent of Poe's famous poem, "The Raven," along with the photo, copies of articles about him, playbills, flyers, and endorsements. "An inexpensive promotional item helps your release stick in the mind of the editor," he says.

CHAPTER 6

Letters That Pitch for You, Rattle the Public, or Roll Out Your Message

If you're targeting just a few media outlets, should you still bother with the formality of a press release? Yes; it contains all the information they need in a format that enables them to appraise it quickly. But if you have some personal connection with a publication or radio/TV program, you may want to use a more personalized approach. Perhaps your college alumni notes inform you that a classmate hosts a talk show, your friend Franny's uncle lives next door to Rudy Reporter, or you once shook hands with the *Sentinel*'s lifestyles editor after hearing her speak. Or perhaps you've read Carole Columnist for ten years and feel as if you know her. In these kinds of cases, send a one-of-a-kind missive likely to be read with more attention, a pitch letter.

Whatever the connection, you lead off a customized pitch letter with a short statement of the link. Then concisely make your pitch, develop it, explain your qualifications on the topic of your pitch, and close the letter. Since you'll need more than a couple of paragraphs to fit all those ingredients, type the letter in standard business-letter format. Either use a letterhead or include your address and phone number at the outset. Here's a successful sample, slightly shortened and edited.

Szifra Birke, M.S., C.A.D.A.C.
One Olde North Road, Suite 304
Chelmsford, MA 01824
(508)250-1554

January 13, 1993

Paul Sullivan
WLLH Radio
44 Church St.
Lowell, MA 01853

Dear Paul,

By way of introduction, I'm Sally's daughter, from the noted Birke's Department Store which after a mere 45 years in business now allows browsing! Your segments have brought my mother lots of attention. It's been fun to watch her reactions. Thanks.

I have a proposal for a show about Children of Alcoholism and Codependency to coincide with National Children of Alcoholics Week, Feb. 14–20, 1993. I hope you would be interested in doing an interview or somehow covering the issue. Besides the national scope, I've enclosed information about a Lowell-area poster contest and other local events scheduled for that week.

According to national estimates, seven million children in the United States are living with at least one alcoholic parent, one of every eight school-aged children. Daily these youngsters face the fear, tension and problems caused by parental drinking and codependency: they are children at risk. Possible angles:
• Bill Clinton was raised in a home with alcoholism.
• "Overage drinking" has as much impact on kids as teenaged drinking. The consistent focus has been adults

advising kids, "Just say no." "Don't you ever do drugs."
Kids need models, not critics.
• Most resilient adults who grew up in alcoholic, troubled
families can point to a person who believed in them—a
grandparent, teacher, coach, clergy, Scout leader. A gift of
attention or love from one of these adults to a child can
change that child's future.
• Many believe that children are fine once their parents are
in recovery. But unless someone addresses their concern that
the parents will start drinking or using again, the children's
worry and hypervigilance will persist.

I have coauthored *Together We Heal: A Real-Life Portrait of
Group Therapy for Adult Children* (Ballantine) and my articles
on identifying and helping children of alcoholics will soon
appear in the teaching magazines *Momentum* and *Teaching
Today.* I am a mental health and alcohol counselor in private
practice in Chelmsford, having begun my work with families of
alcoholics in 1979.

Please let me know if this is a subject of interest to you; and if
you can't use the ideas now, you might consider a story during
Alcohol Awareness Month in April.

Thank you so much for your time.

Sincerely,

Szifra Birke, M.S., C.A.D.A.C.
(My name just looks difficult—it's pronounced "Shifra.")

I don't recommend making up a connection where none ex-
ists, for instance by saying you read or listen to them regularly
when you do not. Not only are the media's BS detectors the best
in the world, suppose your correspondent called you up and
asked you something you could answer only from genuine familiarity with his or her work? Hence even though your computer
makes it easy for you to stick different editors' and producers'
names and addresses into a standard letter, that doesn't count as
meaningfully customizing it.

Another publicity strategy involving a customized pitch letter is agreeing or disagreeing with a newspaper or magazine columnist. Here you latch onto a statement that the columnist has already made and connect your expertise, experience, or convictions to an angle the columnist apparently hadn't considered. Your purpose is to provide corrective information or a challenging viewpoint that inspires or goads the columnist into mentioning you and your point in a future column. Whether you're writing to agree or disagree, maintain a respectful tone. Keep to one or two pages, enclosing supplementary materials you may have that back up your claims and introduce your work or organization more fully. The following is a sample letter I've been tempted to send.

Marcia Yudkin, Ph.D.
Creative Ways
P.O. Box 1310
Boston, MA 02117
(617)266-1613

Thomas Thompson, "Smarter & Smarter"
c/o *Big City Chronicle*
2578 Main Street
Big City, ST 55555

Dear Mr. Thompson:

I read your October 15 column with great interest. As a creativity consultant who teaches productive work habits, I have found that mindmapping is indeed a useful organizational or memory aid—for some people. Using bright-colored markers and a circular, weblike arrangement of ideas does reinforce ideas and make them more memorable for those who are visually oriented. However, we're not all the same. People who are auditorily oriented may need to sort through and absorb material by talking it through with another person, while kinesthetically oriented people learn and remember best by using the material—putting it to work experientially.

I'd be glad to provide further information on creative styles, including additional experts in this area you could speak with, if you are interested. Enclosed are two columns I wrote on discovering one's idiosyncratic creative preferences for *New Writer's Magazine*.

Cordially,

Marcia Yudkin, Ph.D.

In a third strategy involving customized pitch letters, you don't have to wait until a media outlet runs a story relevant to your purpose. You simply write to introduce yourself as a general source on a topic. Since this might not be acted upon right away, if possible send a rotary file card indexed by your topic with your name, affiliation, and phone number along with your letter. Here's how this sort of introductory letter might run:

[on organizational letterhead]

Willa Chu, Producer
WWWW-TV
45 Big Boulevard
Metropolis, ST 29999

Dear Ms. Chu:

If we can predict the future from the past, this summer the abortion controversy is bound to heat up again. Whether it's clinic blockades, demonstrations, abortion-related violence, or new court decisions, you'll probably be looking for a fresh point of view on this seemingly intractable issue. Our group, Women for Dialogue, represents more than 700 women in the greater Metropolis area, both pro-choice and pro-life, who believe in and promote mutual respect and civil debate on abortion.

I would be glad to appear on your show and discuss how productive dialogue on abortion is possible even when opponents are passionate about their positions. Or, I could recommend two of our most articulate members, one on each side, to demonstrate this sort of discussion and interact with callers.

Please call me for more information or if you would like to
arrange for us to appear on your show.

Sincerely,

Patricia James
President, Women for Dialogue

While pitch letters are not designed to be published, another
species of letter is—the Letter to the Editor. Perhaps your junior
high school civics teacher told you that the "Letters" column of
your local newspaper represented democracy and freedom of
the press in action. That's true, but she probably didn't tell you
that the "Letters to the Editor" section of any magazine or newspaper also contains opportunities for free publicity for media-
smart entrepreneurs and professionals. And if you do have
fervent views, or a cause to promote, why sound off only to the
people you know when the media can carry your opinions to
thousands or millions at once?

Basic Facts About Letters to the Editor

Newspapers, which run letters to the editor either right on
their editorial page or very close by, usually offer readers a forum for topics of general concern as well as an opportunity to
respond to articles they published. For example, if you're upset
about the demonstrators who made you late for a job interview,
a newspaper letters column might print your complaint even if
the paper hadn't covered the demonstration. In contrast, most
magazines run letters from readers in a special department up
front and stick to letters that respond to articles that appeared
in recent issues. To contribute a letter to the editor to a magazine, then, you must read the magazine regularly and move
quickly when you spot an opportunity. Unlike call-in radio or TV
shows, which ask you only for your first name and hometown,
both newspapers and magazines customarily publish at least the
letter writer's whole name and hometown, and often an organizational or business affiliation and title as well. And therein lie

chances to get your business message across to prime prospects at no cost to you.

Letters to the editor follow a simple format. Begin with "To the Editor:" even when you know the name of the editor. When responding to a published article, include the title and date of the article prompting your missive in the first sentence or two, in parentheses. Then agree, disagree, correct, comment, or amplify on the content of that article. When sounding off without specific provocation, include an indication of your topic's timeliness right up front before developing your idea. Here, for example, are some model openers:

- "I couldn't agree more with Helen Jay's criticisms of the usual approaches to total quality management ('TQM: Harbinger or Hoax?' October) . . ."
- "Your article 'Lawyers: Lowest of the Low to Some People' (March 28) did a real disservice to the 17.5 percent of attorneys in this county who provide at least some legal services without charge . . ."
- "As the summer fireworks season fast approaches, I'd like to share a story with adults and teenagers who think it's fun to defy the state ban on unlicensed fireworks displays. Five years ago my brother Bernie . . ."

Below your signature, type your name, title (if any), affiliation (if any), and hometown, even if that information appears on your letterhead. Most publications require your phone number. Keep the letter to three paragraphs (250–300 words) to maximize the odds that the publication will run it exactly as you wrote it. Make just one central point in the letter, back it up, and if your purpose is professional visibility, emphasize your credentials within the body of the letter, not only at the end. For example:

- "As inventor of a patented automatic umbrella-drying device, I would like to defend umbrella owners . . ."
- "As someone who began working for animal rights in 1965, I have been gratified by the ever-increasing awareness of human abuses of animals . . ."

- "As a dermatologist who has treated hundreds of cases of severe acne, I disagree that parents should ..."

Stay on the lookout for these five kinds of opportunities to write publishable letters to the editor:

1. *If you agree with a writer.* Don't simply express agreement. Add some information of value that shows off your services, products, programs, or general expertise.

2. *If you disagree.* Even if you're ticked off, keep an even tone and explain why you think the writer was wrong. Insert some facts in your discussion that put your business or organization in a positive light for potential clients.

3. *If you're mentioned in an article and everything is accurate.* Get double mileage from your good fortune by writing a letter of thanks for the mention and making a brief point that wasn't in the original article.

4. *If something in an article requires correction.* Since some readers will read your letter who missed the article you're responding to, never specifically repeat any damaging information or unfavorable claims, even to refute them. Simply set the record straight, and reiterate the basic mission of your business or organization.

5. *If an article overlooked you or your business.* Instead of sulking when an article mentions a competitor, horn in on their good luck. Use the fact that the publication covered your topic as an excuse to bring your existence to the attention of readers. If the article implied that your competitor had the field to itself, gently protest. Otherwise just follow the guidelines above in agreeing or disagreeing with an article.

A Letter to the Editor Success Story

In April 1989, *Inc.* magazine featured an article touting the entrepreneurs it most admired. As Joline Godfrey, then co-owner of Odysseum, a Massachusetts learning-games company, read about *Inc.*'s entrepreneurial "Dream Team," she couldn't help noticing that it included only white males. She got mad enough to sit down and write a letter to the editor, which began:

> "*Inc.*, you let me down. Only ten years old and already smug, self-satisfied, ossified. Four years ago I flexed my entrepreneurial muscle and joined the adventure—started a company and became one of your regular readers. You've kept me abreast of who's doing what, offered up good ideas, cautionary tales, and management visions I can be comfortable with. You've been a pal.

> "But lately I've felt more irked than inspired, more bored than buoyed. Unable to put my finger on just what's wrong, I've remained loyal, reading each issue, trying to understand my discomfort. Then you sent me your anniversary issue. And in one of those awful, illuminating flashes, I got it. *Inc.*, my modern pal, my new age partner, my old friend, you're sexist . . ."

Godfrey went on to document her case. Then, after sending off her letter, she went back to work. Two weeks later, the editor-in-chief of *Inc.*, George Gendron, invited her to lunch to discuss the issues she'd brought up in her letter. Not long after that, Gendron and a colleague interviewed her for a question-and-answer feature in the magazine. Feeling that the deeper reasons for women entrepreneurs' invisibility had yet to be fully exposed, however, she persuaded *Inc.* to help her organize informal dinners for women business owners in four different cities. To explain what she found out, she got a contract for and published her first book, *Our Wildest Dreams: Women Entrepreneurs Making Money, Having Fun, Doing Good.* Not only did her peeved letter provide the material for an influential book, it led Godfrey to a new venture, An Income of Her Own, which provides entrepreneurial education for teenage women. "Never forget the power of the pen and the power of your voice," Joline Godfrey suggests. "Start from the assumption that anything is possible."

CHAPTER 7

Tip Sheets That Keep You in People's Minds— and Files

I wonder if it was a printing company that surreptitiously made business cards de rigueur. Sure, they fit nicely in a suit pocket, but except for the design and a slogan or list of services, they don't offer much of a chance to get your message across. I've managed quite well without cards for a few years, and don't save very many of those that I receive. I did recently, however, run across a sheet of paper titled "How to Produce Photos with Impact" from Nat Starr Associates of Troy, Michigan, that I had picked up at a speakers' convention four or five years ago. Because it was packed with useful tips, I saved it as I wouldn't have Starr's business card or brochure. You may not want to dispense with cards, but I hope you'll consider keeping tip sheets on hand along with the stationery, cards, and brochures in your supply closet.

Introducing the Tip Sheet

A tip sheet is basically a list of generally six to fifteen tips that show off your expertise and explain to the reader how to solve a personal or professional problem. The title should clearly indicate the content, and there should be an introduction of one to four paragraphs, followed by the numbered tips. Generally a tip sheet consists of only one page, written in a crisp, readable style.

The title serves to arouse interest among exactly the people you hope will become patrons of your business. Alliteration ("Five Factors"), surprise, and zippy numbers—eight and twelve have more snazz than nine or eleven—add appeal. These sample titles would work for tip sheets:

- 12 Ways to Save on Property Taxes—Legally
- How to Catch a Rich Husband in Less Than a Year
- Five Factors to Consider Before Choosing a Physician
- What You Should Know About Stockbrokers and Why
- Why Most Quality-Control Programs Don't Work
- How to Check Out Your Dream House Before You Buy It
- Eight Ways to Improve Your Golf Game—Off the Course

The following would not work for a tip sheet:

- 17 Reasons Hanrahan, Hanrahan, and O'Reilly Should Become Your Law Firm

Remember that a tip sheet is not blatant self-promotion. A good one promotes you in a subtle but compelling way because it offers information that only someone with genuine expertise could have delivered. It can contain examples, stories, or cases that embody what you've done for others, but these are always subordinate to the tips. Use this question to distinguish an effective tip sheet from a marketing piece in the format of a tip sheet: Would this information be helpful to someone in my target market who couldn't care less about me and who might not ever buy my products or services? If the answer is yes, you're on the right track.

Because a tip sheet may have a long drawer life, it must be impeccably written. Polish it, edit it, and proofread carefully. Unless you were an English major in college, find someone professional to go over it and make sure spelling, punctuation, and grammar are correct and consistent.

At a minimum, include your contact information prominently on the tip sheet. You can also soft-sell yourself on the tip sheet in a final paragraph that combines biographical information with what you offer clients and customers and how to get in touch with you.

It will look more official and impressive if you typeset your tip sheet in two or three columns. Most printing and quick-copy shops can do this for you for a reasonable fee. "Make it easy to read, so that you can take in what it is at a glance," says Barbara Winter of Minneapolis, who recommends tip sheets in the workshop she teaches around the country, "How to Establish Yourself as an Expert." "Don't worry about making it slick and glossy. I've seen excellent tip sheets printed on a letterhead," says Winter.

How to Use Tip Sheets

Let's count the ways tip sheets can earn you free publicity.

1. *A black-and-white proof of your expertise.* Until you sit down to write your first tip sheet, you may not realize how much you know. "When you choose a small subject and decide to collect eight to ten important points about it, that forces you to slow down and get organized. Then that builds your confidence," says Barbara Winter. It also builds up confidence among reporters and producers that you know your stuff. As a component of your press kit, a well-done tip sheet lends you at least as much added credibility as a photocopied clipping of an article by you in a nonprestigious publication.

2. *A handout that you provide at seminars or meetings.* Unlike your talk, a tip sheet can be referred to again and again and

passed on to others. The audience appreciates having the highlights of the presentation or additional pointers in a format that's much neater than their own notes. After the talk, the organization you spoke to might reprint your tip sheet in its newsletter. Tip sheets come in especially handy on those occasions when you're speaking and the organization discourages you from selling products, giving your services a plug, or even passing out business cards. No one ever objects when you pass out beneficial information, and right there at the bottom is how to get in touch with you.

You can pass out tip sheets anywhere prospects have gathered, not only when you're up on the podium as the star. Enterprising folks have placed them on literature tables or handed them out personally at trade shows and exhibitions. People will pick them up and keep them when they would not hang onto brochures or simple advertising flyers.

3. *Material that you offer as a "freebie" to attract and identify potential customers.* My most-used tip sheet originated in an article on getting published in big-circulation magazines. I wrote it for a writers' newsletter called *Minnesota Ink*, and it was later reprinted in the newsletter of the Boston local of the National Writers Union, to which I belong. Shortly afterwards, I transformed this article into a tip sheet and used it in a way that has worked for me many times since then. Having noticed that the Writers Digest Book Club bulletin included a column in which members asked other members for help or offered it, I wrote in announcing the availability of a free special report called "Breaking into Major Magazines." To those who sent me their self-addressed stamped envelope after the club ran my notice, I sent my tip sheet along with a flyer for my *Freelance Writing* book and a promotional piece about my consulting services. One respondent from that promotion has remained a valuable client three years later.

Many, many publications are delighted to run freebie notices at no cost to you. This is a tremendous deal, considering the credibility you receive because the offer isn't framed as an ad and the fact that your costs only include copying and some time stuffing envelopes. Carefully select publications whose readers would benefit from your tips and send them either a press release about the offer or a business letter plus a sample of the tip sheet.

4. *Something you can send off to be published.* Whenever you compile and print up a new tip sheet, let it do double duty by submitting it to pertinent publications. Make sure you only sell or give away so-called "one-time rights" rather than "all rights" so that you can continue to use your tip sheet in all the other ways on this list. Insist that the publication include your contact information at the end of the tips. If you offer the piece for free, it's especially hard for them to refuse.

5. *Use a tip sheet as a panel of a brochure.* Barbara Winter recalls a wedding consultant who took her advice and incorporated a list called "10 Ways to Have a Smoother Wedding" into her brochure. "People are more likely to hang on to your advertising piece when it includes valuable information that makes it more than advertising," she says. "I have a drawer loaded with little pamphlets on how to tie a scarf, take care of silk, decorate with baskets, and buy a new car."

Beyond One-Pagers

This chapter spent its first life as a tip sheet. At 853 words, it fit easily and nicely onto one page. If you could match that and develop sixty-nine more tip sheets around the same size, *voilà*, you'd have a full-length book. Or just double the length and use larger type, and you could have a four-page booklet. With at least four pages of tip-sheet-type information, you can even charge a dollar or two to defray your copying costs. New Jersey–based writer Robert Bly once charged as much as $7.00 for a booklet called "Recession-Proof Business Strategies: 14 Winning Methods to Sell Any Product or Service in a Down Economy," and sold more than 3,000 entirely through press releases to business magazines and newspapers. In case your math is rusty, that's a gross of $21,000. "The topic was timely," he explains in his book, *Targeted Public Relations*. "The release was issued during the worst of the recession of the early 1990s."

The book you are reading now originated as a booklet. For a

seminar I taught, I had created a four-page handout called "Six Steps to Free Publicity" and printed it up in an 11" by 17" folded format. Then I thought, How can I use this to bring in additional business? I tried to sell it from a classified ad in *Entrepreneur*, but that didn't break even. I offered it for free to members of the National Speakers Association through their membership newsletter. Close to one hundred asked for the booklet, but none bought audiotapes or expressed interest in my consulting services. Not giving up, I offered it to the national newsletter *Bottom Line/Personal* for its "Freebies" column. At no cost to me, it ran six small lines describing the booklet and how to send for it. A staff person called me shortly before the notice ran to make sure I had 500 booklets on hand to satisfy anticipated demand.

Five hundred sounded like a lot to me, but I passed that number five days after the first self-addressed stamped envelopes started to arrive. Then a blizzard shut down the post office, I had to go to New York for a day, and I returned to find 700 more requests waiting for me. And they kept on arriving. A postal clerk told me, as he fetched my daily bucket or two of envelopes, that I was receiving more volume than some of the mammoth companies that got their mail at that station. My husband set up an efficient system for the two of us to open the envelopes, type the names into the computer, fold the booklet together with my follow-up materials, and stuff and send them all off within a few days of receipt. When three weeks had gone by, we had received 3,000 requests and given my printer a Christmas bonus's worth of unanticipated business. And luckily, product orders and consulting jobs were beginning to bounce back.

By the end of the second month, I had a good idea of who the 4,300 people were who'd written and why, and I wrote a book proposal. Without this bonanza, I'm sure I wouldn't have stopped to think whether I knew enough about the subject to write a good book. Nor would I have had quite enough credibility to make the case that I was someone who could get people to buy the book. But I explained to publishers that because of the free publicity I'd received from *Bottom Line/Personal*, I now had a proven title and free market research on the kinds of people who were interested in free publicity. Of course, I had also amassed a list of prime customers for the book. When I began negotiating a contract with Plume Books, I was still receiving an average of twenty requests a week. The moral, I suppose, is to watch what you wish for; you might get a dozen times more!

CHAPTER 8

Painlessly Publishing
Articles Yourself

Publish? Me? I barely passed ninth-grade English!

Never mind. If you can create a list of useful tips, you can write a publishable magazine article. Getting published on your own is the fastest way to establish yourself as an expert; it helps you reach out to your target market; and it keeps on working for you forever when you include copies of your publications in your press kit or send them out to potential clients. In comparison with courting the media through press releases, you have more control of your message through article writing. You'll also have the opportunity to develop your ideas in more depth.

Two major routes to publication exist: submitting a completed article, and sending a query letter that proposes an article. It may surprise you to learn that the latter is the more common route to publication. But both strategies work, and I'll describe the steps involved in each.

Getting Focused

Both strategies begin with market research. Before you set pen to paper or fingers to the keyboard, decide on your market, the group of people you'd like to reach. Here are some sample markets:

- Women with enough wealth to afford diamonds
- Utility contractors who might need legal advice
- CEOs in the West
- Travel agents that sell cruises
- Training directors of companies with more than 500 employees

At this stage, keep your publicity goal explicitly in mind. If you're writing articles to bring in new business, don't direct your writing toward your peers—other accountants, printers, restaurateurs—but toward your potential clients or customers. If you're hoping to get referrals from other physicians, roofers, or boat charterers who don't handle the specialized tasks you do, however, writing for your own professional or trade group makes good sense. With a goal of winning new converts to recycling, don't target a group that's probably already convinced. But with a goal of recruiting volunteers and donors for your nonprofit recycling initiative, by all means reach out to the converted.

After defining your market, think about and investigate what periodicals people in your target market read. The more specifically you've zeroed in on a target group, the more specialized should be the publications you approach. Then visit your public library, which contains numerous guides to publications of many types. Think about these nine categories of periodicals:

1. *Trade magazines.* Oriented toward practitioners of a narrowly defined business or profession, these magazines are rarely familiar to outsiders. But you'll find them listed in *Writer's Market, Gale Directory of Publications and Broadcast Media,* and the *Standard Periodical Directory.*

2. *Regional business papers and magazines.* Examples: *San Diego Business Journal, Business Atlanta, New England Business.* These cover business and economic news in a defined geographic area. Make sure you have a local angle for this sort of periodical, and then check the listings in the *Gale Directory of Publications and Broadcast Media, Editor and Publisher International Yearbook, Bacon's Magazine Directory, Working Press of the Nation, Volume 1* or the *Standard Rate and Data Service Business Publications Directory.*

3. *City newspapers.* Even the most casual visitor to your area soon learns the name of your city newspaper—the one sold in all the convenience stores and delivered to doorsteps and special colored mailboxes. In addition, there are *USA Today* and the *Wall Street Journal,* two national newspapers. Larger papers have special sections for different topics, including food, entertainment, science, and education, and many accept contributions from people besides their salaried reporters. Look up newspapers outside your area in *Editor and Publisher International Yearbook* or *Bacon's Newspaper Directory.*

4. *Shoppers and community newspapers.* These free tabloid-sized newspapers come to your house or sit stacked ready for pickup at neighborhood supermarkets, libraries, and newsstands. Some include little but ads, while others contain local features and useful information for a broad base of local readers. They may be open to "how-to" articles on plumbing, real estate, cooking, or other subjects of general interest. Stick to those you can easily collect where you live and work.

5. *Alternative newspapers.* Some of these fall under the above heading, since they're stacked around for free pickup, but some cost from 50 cents to $1.50 at newsstands. Many include calendar listings. In my area, we have the *Boston Phoenix,* which covers politics, the arts, and lifestyles; *The Improper Bostonian,* an arts and entertainment biweekly for young professionals; and *EarthStar,* a bimonthly guide for the spiritually minded distributed at New Age bookstores, health food stores, and office buildings. Michael Levine offers a list of thirty-two of these publications from major cities in the appendix of his book, *Guerrilla P.R.*

6. *Association magazines and newsletters.* Many trade, cultural, and activist organizations publish periodicals for their

members. Look up any subject from abuse and neglect to zeppe-
lins in your library's copy of the *Encyclopedia of Associations*
to locate prime candidates for your articles.

7. *Subscription newsletters.* People buy subscriptions to
these newsletters rather than receive them along with membership in an organization, and they're listed in the *Oxbridge Directory of Newsletters*, *Newsletters in Print*, and *Hudson's
Newsletter Directory.* Often the publisher/editor writes the entire newsletter, but some subscription newsletters include material from outside contributors.

8. *Consumer magazines.* People buy consumer magazines
for enjoyment and for information on hobbies, travel, people,
and well-being. Readers usually comprise a distinct demo-
graphic subsection of the population, divided by ethnicity, sex,
religion, age, region, or personal interests. The larger the circulation, the harder it will be for you to get articles published in
these outlets; many deal primarily with professional writers.
Look this category up in *Writer's Market* or the *Standard Periodical Directory.*

9. *Academic or scholarly journals.* If you possess proven expertise or academic credentials, try getting your work published
in these volumes, which expect footnotes and other scholarly
appurtenances. *Ulrich's International Periodical Directory* and
the *Standard Periodical Directory* provide a guide for all subject areas.

For the examples I cited earlier, research would lead you to
some of these periodicals:

- Women with enough wealth to afford diamonds: *Lear's;
  Town and Country; Architectural Digest*
- Utility contractors who might need legal advice: *National
  Utility Contractor; Pipeline & Underground Utilities
  Construction*
- CEOs in the West: *Boulder County Business Report; Cali-
  fornia Business; Oregon Business; San Francisco Busi-
  ness Times*
- Travel agents that sell cruises: *Star Service; Sailaway*
- Training directors of companies with more than 500 em-
  ployees: *Human Resource Executive; Training*

After you've selected a target publication, decide what kind of article would be in line with your goal. Here are four kinds of articles that can serve as a vehicle for publicity:

1. *An opinion piece.* Journalists call these "op-ed" pieces because they often appear in newspapers *op*posite the *ed*itorial page. Magazines of all sorts run them, too. More carefully crafted than letters to the editor, these short pieces should be carefully reasoned and supported with persuasive evidence. Timeliness counts, but that includes tying your point of view in with general trends as well as with front-page news or holidays. Consultant Alan Weiss makes his submissions stand out by taking an opposite tack on hot topics. When the business world was excited about "quality," he wrote "The Myth of Quality Circles," and when "managing diversity" became a catchphrase, he succeeded with the theme, "Don't manage diversity, embrace it."

2. *A personal experience piece.* Writing about your feelings and experiences and observations may seem an odd route to publicity, but it pays off all the time for people seeking publishers or literary agents. I see no reason why a personal essay couldn't lure customers and clients if placed in the right publication. Examples of topics and publications would include a divorce attorney reflecting on the sadness and hope of his profession for a women's magazine, or an ice cream store owner writing for a city parents' magazine about the experience of serving kids in the town where she grew up. A memorable personal experience piece includes depth of feeling and dramatic detail.

3. *A "how-to" or service piece.* See Chapter 7 on how to create a tip sheet that is also publishable as an article. Instead of six or eight or twelve separate tips, you can also provide a series of steps that explain a process, or even just elaborate on one solution to a common problem. Whenever you tie your advice to pressing needs of a publication's readers, you'll meet with great demand. Include examples that show off your problem-solving prowess but avoid a self-promotional tone.

4. *A round-up.* If you can't come up with enough stories and tips to fill an article, interview more seasoned experts and create a collage of their advice. The multiple voices cut down on the credibility and visibility you earn with this kind of article,

but you will come off as well informed and the piece offers a grand excuse for networking through phone interviews with the greats in your field.

After deciding on a type of article, choose a subject. If you're just starting out, keep your focus very practical and specific.

Brainstorm what some of your major points about that subject might be. Then either organize those thoughts into an outline of the article or use them to write a query letter, following the instructions below.

If You Write a Completed Article

Polish your piece and make sure it's the right length for your target publication. Type it or print it out in the format of the sample on pages 85–86—double-spaced, with wide margins on all sides and your name, address, telephone number, social security number (for markets that pay), and approximate word count on the top of the first page. Head subsequent pages with your last name and the page number in the upper right-hand corner. Include a biographical sentence or two at the end of the manuscript with enough contact information for readers to easily find you. Although some determined readers will track you down without contact information accompanying the article, you'll get a greater response if the publication says where you live or, even better, your address and phone number. Keeping a copy for yourself, send the article together with a short cover letter offering "one-time rights" to the piece, along with a biographical paragraph explaining your credentials to write the piece. ("One-time rights" means the publication has the right to publish your piece once, with you retaining all other rights.) Enclose a self-addressed stamped envelope and wait a minimum of six weeks before following up with a polite inquiry if you haven't received a reply. Most editors will eventually answer you, and send you a sample copy of the publication with your article if they do use it.

Should you expect payment? I have mixed feelings on this issue. As someone who has made a living from writing for more than thirteen years and who supports efforts to improve working conditions for writers, I believe that writing articles is work that deserves reasonable payment and respectful treatment. However, as someone advising you on how to get free publicity through writing, I have to tell you that some magazines and newspapers will find room for your work more readily if you offer an article for free. Indeed, I was once asked to serve as an expert witness in a case where a business tabloid viewed publication in exchange for publicity as a fair quid pro quo. They even sent two editors to court for three whole days to wait for the case to come up. I was on the side of the freelancer, who won by showing the judge that the paper had told *Writer's Market* that it paid $150–$225 for contributions. Yet to complicate the matter further, at the higher-quality, higher-budget publications, such as *Working Woman* or the *Wall Street Journal*, you would undercut your credibility by saying you were willing to forego payment. Perhaps the best policy would be to say in your cover letter that you're offering the article "on your usual terms," which leaves them the opening to tell you what their usual terms are.

Article fees, where they exist, vary widely. There are no standard rates. You may receive anything from an honorarium of $25 to $1,000 for a 1,000-word article (about four pages). After you receive sample copies, cut out your article, eliminating any advertisements that may share the pages, and paste it up nicely. You'll now have an impressive clip for your press kit.

Sample Manuscript Format

First page

Jane Author
368 Any Street
Maintown, ST 00000
(555)555-5555

Approx. 1,200 words
One-time rights
S.S. #888-88-8888

TITLE SHOULD BE CENTERED
by Jane Author

Then start the manuscript itself here and continue until the end in double spacing.

Subsequent pages

Author 2

Then just continue here after the author's name/page number slug in the upper right corner.

Sample Cover Letter When Submitting a Completed Article

Jane Author, CPA
368 Any Street
Maintown, ST 00000
(555)555-5555

Edmund Editor
Manhattan Magazine
792 Manhattan Avenue
New York, NY 10000

Dear Mr. Editor:

Enclosed is a 700-word article entitled "Twelve (Mostly) New Ways to Beat the Tax Man." Four of the twelve tips remind readers of steps they need to take in December before the tax year ends, while the other eight present fresh ideas they should discuss with their accountants before tax time.

The article comes out of my eighteen years of experience as an accountant specializing in personal finance and three months of intensive study of loopholes and opportunities in new tax regulations. I am a frequent guest on the WFPK radio show *Mainline to Money*, which airs Fridays at 5:00 P.M.

I look forward to hearing whether or not you'd like to
piece and if so, on what terms.

Sincerely,

Jane Author, CPA

If You Send a Query

Most editors prefer queries because a short proposal allows
them to provide you with input that ensures the length and the
slant that they want. However, writing effective queries takes a
little study and practice. Editors will have three questions in
mind when they read your query:

- What specifically is this person proposing to write?
- Is this for us?
- Can this person write?

Bolster your chances of receiving a go-ahead for the article
by heeding these guidelines:

1. Address the query to a specific editor by name. Get the
name from *Writer's Market*, the other periodical directories
listed earlier in this chapter, or from the list of editors inside the
magazine.

2. Keep it to one page if possible.

3. Use a personal letterhead or include your address and
phone number at the top of the letter.

4. The letter must showcase your writing ability and evidence
a mastery of spelling, punctuation, and grammar. The writing
style must be compatible with that of the magazine you're que-
rying.

5. One option: write the first paragraph of the query letter as
if it were the first paragraph of the article. Begin with an anec-
dote, startling statistic, interesting examples, or sparkling description.

6. Include the specific focus of the article and explain how

you'll handle the topic. Naming one or two sources of information never hurts.

7. End with selected biographical information, including previous publications (if any), and any personal or professional facts that bolster your credibility to write on the topic.

8. Don't give everything away in the letter, but make it sound as if you already know a lot about your topic.

9. Enclose a self-addressed stamped envelope.

As with a completed article, wait about six weeks before calling or writing to follow up. You have the right to send the same or a similar query to several publications at the same time.

Sample Article Query

[on letterhead stationery]

December 12, 1990

Wendy Myers, Editor
Women in Business
9100 Ward Parkway
Kansas City, MO 64114

Dear Ms. Myers:

"HUMBLE CREATIVITY FOR GRAND RESULTS:
10 Little Things That Help Your Work Stand Out"

Marcel Proust could write only in a cork-lined room. Isadora Duncan would stand immobile for hours, waiting for contact with "the music of the soul." Thomas Edison found the right material for his light-bulb filament after trying and discarding a numbing 7,034 other possibilities. Although the most widespread folklore about creativity comes from stories about famous artists and inventors, I propose an article about how ordinary businesswomen can increase their everyday originality without heroics.

After a short lead, I'll discuss ten easy creativity boosters that help one break out of ruts and freshen up routine ideas. They will include:

- Honoring your body rhythms. Concentration peaks when you schedule demanding work for your prime thinking hours, which differ from person to person. For maximum productivity, it's also vital to take breaks at least every ninety minutes.
- Generating lots of ideas. At formal brainstorming sessions, unexpected ideas surface after the more predictable ones. Unless you go beyond the first, second and third possibilities that occur to you, you'll be repeating the usual kinds of solutions.
- Finding gems in the trash. Instead of tossing out schemes that obviously couldn't work, ask, "What's right about it?" When a bad idea is dusted off and twisted a little, it can begin to shine.

I'll illustrate my suggestions with numerous examples from working women.

In addition to being Vice-President of WordRight, a consulting firm that presents writing seminars to businesses, I am at work on my fifth book, on creativity. *Smart Speaking: Sixty-Second Strategies*, which I coauthored with Laurie Schloff, will appear from Henry Holt in April 1991, with excerpts scheduled to appear in *Cosmopolitan, Ladies Home Journal,* and *Woman's Day.* My articles have also appeared in the *New York Times, Psychology Today, Barrister, Computer Update, MD,* and elsewhere. Enclosed is a sample article that appeared in *TWA Ambassador.*

I look forward to hearing from you.

Yours,

Marcia Yudkin

On Beyond Articles

The ultimate publicity value from writing accompanies publishing a book. According to Larry Rochester, author of *Book Publicity for Authors and Publishers,* the greater media attention paid to authors than nonauthors has a logical explanation. Media people assume that anyone who has published a book has researched a subject thoroughly and thus can probably speak with authority and passion on his or her subject. Even when a topic isn't directly related to the book you've published, doors can open. I experienced a strange confirmation of this principle after I wrote a pitch letter about my work on creativity to a business writer named Michael Pellecchia, whose column gets picked up by newspapers around the country after it appears in the *Fort Worth Star-Telegram.* After interviewing me by mail and phone, he told me that since his column featured business books, he would mention the forthcoming paperback edition of *Smart Speaking* in the opening before turning to my ideas on creativity, which I was currently researching and teaching about. In other words, the fact that I had published a book made me eligible for coverage on a completely different topic in his column.

Another publicity advantage of books over articles is that a book that lives on in libraries can keep your name before editors, producers, and the public forever. More than a decade after its publication, social worker Merle Bombardieri was still receiving calls from potential clients who had found her 1981 book, *The Baby Decision,* in their public library. She also received a call from Ande Zellman, editor of the *Boston Globe Magazine,* who asked how she could get a copy of *The Baby Decision,* which was out of print, for the *Globe Magazine* library. Bombardieri had been quoted a few times in the magazine, but she'd never written for it herself. Thinking quickly, she asked Zellman, "While I have you on the phone, are you the right person to send queries to?" Zellman replied, "Yes, but why don't you tell me what you had in mind to write?" Bombardieri made up an article idea that capitalized on the editor's interest in her book and received a contract for her ad-libbed idea in the mail.

Finally, even in this electronic age, the depth of knowledge revealed in a book can make a direct, gratifying impact on readers. Tony Putman says that since publishing *Marketing Your Services,* he's received telephone calls and letters from every continent except Antarctica, representing hundreds of thousands of dollars in billings. The secret, he says, is writing something that makes a clear and distinctive point about the difference you can make with the problems readers have. "Write so that the reader will say, 'This is exactly what I've been looking for. I'll give this person a call' "—excellent advice to keep in mind for articles, too.

CHAPTER 9

Advertorials That Don't Cost You a Cent

Ever since I can remember reading the Sunday *New York Times*, I've seen copy by Albert Shanker, president of the American Federation of Teachers, in the upper right-hand corner of an inside page of the "News of the Week in Review" section. The capitalized word "Advertisement" above the heading "Where We Stand" signals that Shanker isn't a *Times* editorial writer but that the AFT pays to have his editorial appear in that space. Perhaps a decade ago, I began to notice pages-long article sections in magazines like the *Atlantic Monthly* that were similarly labeled "Advertisement." Often they bore the sponsorship of the tourist boards of various countries, companies manufacturing beauty products, or special-interest groups. More recently still, I learned that a term had been coined for this sort of paid media feature: "advertorial."

As you might guess from the word itself, an advertorial is a hybrid of an advertisement and editorial copy. Written by someone in the pay not of the magazine but of the advertising company, a good advertorial looks like an article and reads like an article. So close are the verbal and visual resemblances, in fact, that most magazines insist on the word "Advertisement" in small print at the top of the advertorial so readers won't hold the magazine responsible for the contents. Those that are well-written and interesting lure readers who may not notice any difference from the publication's regular features or who notice but may not care. Advertorials in this guise can cost more than ten years' worth of your advertising budget. But you can arrange the same kind of impact in all but the very most prestigious publications without paying a cent. Here's how.

An Advertorial by Another Name

Instead of calling it an "advertorial," you call it a "column"—or a "regular column." Choose a publication whose readers constitute a target market, and define a subject area likely to interest that group of people. Low-priced publications such as newsletters and free alternative papers are especially likely to jump at a well-thought-out idea, but trade magazines that reach people in a particular business or profession (*Concrete Dealers' News*, *Lawyers' Monthly*) can be receptive, too.

Linda Marks, a body-centered psychotherapist in Newton, Massachusetts, writes a regular column for *Spirit of Change*, a free quarterly on holistic healing and New Age ideas that is distributed in bookstores, libraries, and health food stores throughout much of New England. At the end of her column, which spans two pages, the paper lists her credentials, her special area of expertise, her book *Living with Vision*, and her phone number. Accompanying the second page of the article is a 5″ by 5″ advertisement for Marks's programs. Note that it would be prohibitively expensive for her to run a two-page ad, but by combining an article on subjects of interest to her readers with a traditional-looking ad, she gets great double exposure, and much more credibility than if she only had an ad.

To maintain the trust of editors and readers, design your column so that it is truly informative rather than a disguised promotional piece. You need a relatively authoritative tone that showcases your expertise, not your opinions. Here are eight more possibilities:

- *For a restaurant:* a healthy-eating column in a local weekly paper or monthly magazine under the by-line of the chef or owner (rather than a collection of recipes from the restaurant, so that the column comes across as a public service)
- *For a hairdresser:* a column in a community paper on cures for common hair problems
- *For a real estate agent:* a column in the local newspaper or magazine for homeowners on ways to enhance and protect the value of their real estate
- *For a museum:* a column in a local paper of historical vignettes from at least fifty years back
- *For an adoption agency:* a column in a national parenting magazine on myths and realities about adoption
- *For a tax lawyer:* a monthly column in the regional business tabloid discussing developments in the tax laws affecting business
- *For an environmental group:* a nature-appreciation column highlighting local scenic sites, flora, and fauna for a community paper
- *For a mail-order office supplies company:* a column on running an efficient office for a trade magazine or newsletter read by secretaries and office managers

An easy format to use consists of questions and answers. In the beginning, of course, you'll have to make up the questions as well as the answers, but the Q&A format invites more reader participation than the usual article style.

Jeffrey Lant has constructed an information-selling empire whose foundation is an advertorial he calls "Sure-Fire Business Success." At last count his column was reaching 1.5 million people per month through more than 200 different publications worldwide and some computer information services. He provides the copy for free in exchange for one hard-sell paragraph at the end of the article that promotes his books and consulting services, as in the following slightly abbreviated example:

Dr. Jeffrey Lant is one of America's most well-known marketers for the single reason that he's unrelentingly focused on doing what it takes to help you sell more of your products and services. Profit from his 480-page book, *Cash*

Copy: How to Offer Your Products and Services So Your Prospects Buy Them . . . Now! ($38.50 postpaid) Get a free year's subscription to his quarterly 32-page "Sure-Fire Business Success Catalog" by contacting JLA Publications, P.O. Box 38–2767, Cambridge, MA 02238, or calling (617) 547–6372.

Lant knows the column works because orders constantly flow in and he receives dozens of calls day and night from readers around the world, many of whom say they feel like they know him. His distinctive voice, that of a blustery, no-nonsense authority, certainly comes across in everything he writes. While imbuing your column with personality helps get reader response, so does a steadfast focus on content that helps readers solve their problems. "If you're a plumber, think of yourself as a specialist with a technical body of expertise that people desperately need when they have a problem," Lant advises. Publishers who carry his column appreciate the fact that he provides twenty-five columns at a whack, on disk, for them to choose from, containing information that will be valid for the foreseeable future and that he is forever recycling and updating.

Jim Cooke, a Boston actor who executed a column on a much smaller scale, was also very satisfied with having done it. To promote his one-man show on Calvin Coolidge, he wrote eighteen free monthly columns on Coolidge for the *Green Mountain Gazette* in Vermont, our thirtieth president's home state. Although he doesn't recall more than a few letters and inquiries about performances, "It helped me develop material," he says, "and I can still send out photocopies of the column. It's worthwhile because you never know where something is going to end up. Someone in a small town in Vermont who read the column sees my name later and says, 'Oh, that's the guy who wrote the column.' It's like a drop of water wearing away a rock. You don't know which drop of water will do it, but it happens."

For Linda Marks, the biggest motivator is the chance her column gives her amidst a busy speaking, teaching, and counseling practice to keep her hand in as a writer. Although she has received some twenty letters or phone calls from readers, that's just a warm, fuzzy bonus for her. Some of the feedback about her column is critical, especially when she writes about what she calls the "dark side" of human nature, and Marks feels fine about that, too. "To be a columnist, you need a point of view," she explains. "Not everyone will like it, but if it has enough substance that people can argue with it, then you have the chance to make a long-term impact. If all you get is positive feedback, you're probably not making a deep enough connection with the reader."

How to Do It

Before contacting an editor to propose a column, write at least one sample column. Send that together with a cover letter that explains the focus and title of your proposed column, the fact that you're offering to do it for free or in exchange for advertising space, and why you are the perfect person to write the column. If that editor doesn't show interest, try another. Remember that when your goal is reader response, the column works best for you if it includes explicit contact information at the end. If the publication's format allows, a photo of you topping the column each time can also promote reader involvement. When your goal is name recognition and reputation-building, give the column at least a year to produce an impact. The more you appear before your audience in your role of expert, the more your advertorial—whoops, column—promotes you.

SPEAKING
AND ACTING
FOR
PUBLICITY

CHAPTER 10

Staging Magnet Events

January 19, 1989, was the 180th anniversary of the birth of Edgar Allan Poe, and Norman George, a Boston actor who portrays Poe in a show called "Poe Alone," was determined to make it a memorable occasion. Because Poe's birthplace, Boston, had treated the author shabbily during his lifetime, George decided that a good media hook would be " 'The Raven' Comes Home to Roost"—with Boston making amends to its famous son. George enlisted Poe scholars, aficionados, and prominent Boston businessmen into a Poe Memorial Committee charged with getting Carver Street, where Poe was born, renamed for Poe. The committee soon succeeded in securing a proclamation from Mayor Ray Flynn, a bronze memorial plaque, and a new street sign marking "Edgar Allan Poe Way." Meanwhile, he planned a slide lecture and benefit performance of his show.

In early October 1988, George mailed a first round of press releases about the celebration to monthly consumer magazines, airline magazines and *Amtrak Express*, detective and mystery magazines, and newsletters and literary journals. He also called or wrote producers and editors and contacted freelance writers he knew who had connections with *People* and *Yankee* magazines. In late December and early January, he sent releases and calendar listings to the Boston-area dailies and weeklies, and TV and radio stations.

The national publicity blitz paid off. Because of pre-event coverage in *Yankee* and the *Boston Globe, Herald, Phoenix*, and *Tab*, among others, a standing-room-only audience of more than 600 people packed into the anniversary performance, and post-event coverage appeared in *People*, the *New York Times*, Associated Press newspapers, and elsewhere. Because of the exposure, theater managers contacted George to book his show, documentary filmmakers and radio producers offered him related roles, and the state of Maryland, where Poe died, conferred honorary citizenship on George. In all, the media-savvy actor estimates that more than ten million people read or heard about the story.

The Attraction of a Magnet Event

In Chapter 2, I suggested that a special event such as a lecture or free demonstration can add timeliness to an otherwise ongoing service or establishment. A magnet event includes some additional component that makes an event irresistible to the media. The extra ingredient might be one of the following:

1. *Celebrities/prominent people.* In Norman George's case, the featured celebrity was a dead one whom most Americans had probably heard of. Although Poe would not attend, George, his reincarnation, would give a speech and intone "The Raven" with the style, costume, and mannerisms Poe was known for. The imprimatur of the mayor didn't hurt, either. Charity hostesses know well that the more glittery and well-known the people who attend their event, the more photos and column inches they're likely to get in the paper afterwards.

2. *Curiosity/suspense.* In 1980 Bob Allen claimed that he could go to any city with $100 and in seventy-two hours would own several properties without using his own money. The *Los Angeles Times* took the bait and challenged him to do it. The free publicity Allen got when he delivered on his boast launched

him as a phenomenon and kept his book *Nothing Down* on the bestseller lists long enough to become the biggest-selling real estate book of all time. The curiosity/suspense factor came in when Allen predicted that he would do it and the *Times* followed him to report on whether or not he could. As any street performer who announces, "And now I'm going to juggle five knives" knows, telling an audience what you're going to do is risky, no matter how many times you've done it while practicing. Even Allen confesses that the days that earned him the headline BUYING HOME WITHOUT CASH: BOASTFUL INVESTOR ACCEPTS TIME CHALLENGE—AND WINS were the most harrowing of his life.

3. *Colorfulness/humor.* Around the time of Bob Allen's exploit, I belonged to a group called Women for Survival that organized an annual Mother's Day march for peace through our town of Northampton, Massachusetts. By mentioning in our press release that the parade would include colorful banners and kids holding balloons, we easily enticed TV reporters and print photographers to show up at the march every year. Similarly, when TV reporters got wind of Ron Bianco running his singing dog Bilbo for president, they knew that the formal kickoff of his candidacy, which Bianco notified them would take place on the lawn of the Rhode Island State House, would be a howler for their viewers.

4. *Uniqueness.* Calculatedly, Jeffrey Lant stressed that no convention of consultants had ever taken place in Boston when he pitched the Boston Consulting Convention he and a colleague sponsored to the media in 1982. Even when it seems a stretch, creating an air of uniqueness can help, as when you're traveling to Chicago to give a speech and bill it as your "first and only Chicago appearance."

5. *Resonance.* According to Nell Merlino, creator and producer of Take Our Daughters to Work Day, some ideas turn into mega-events because they tap into what millions of people are thinking and feeling. "I don't think there's much of a difference between what the media are interested in and what the public is interested in," Merlino says. "Take Our Daughters to Work Day got so much coverage because people working at newspapers and radio stations heard about it and immediately wanted to bring their own daughters to work. Then it was natural for them to want to spread the word."

Danger, Danger

But a magnet event involves much more than sending off a press release. "It takes money, time, creativity, and nerve—all difficult," says Richard Falk, a New York City public relations consultant who holds the distinction of being the first inductee selected for the Press Agents Hall of Fame. Much can go wrong. Ron Bianco spent hundreds of dollars rallying supporters, printing T-shirts, and renting masks, banners, hats, and a police officer for the press conference to be held on the State House lawn in Providence. Then it rained and he had to reschedule. For retailer Rick Segel, a great idea turned into a nightmare. He sponsored a contest for the best hairdresser in Medford, Massachusetts. The first year resulted in a photo of contestants wearing $20,000 worth of fur coats from his store winding up on the front page of the local paper. The second year he expanded the contest, renting a hall and selling 500 tickets. When one contestant complained that the fur coat bearing her contestant number didn't fit, coats and numbers were switched around, but without coordinating that properly with the judges' lists. "As a result, some of the prizes were announced for the wrong people," Segel says. "Two of the judges walked out, and there were practically fistfights among the hairdressers."

Sometimes the idea is so catchy and memorable that it gets separated from the sponsor who is supposed to benefit from the publicity. On retainer for a refrigerator company, publicist Jim Moran proved wrong the saying that you can't sell an icebox to an Eskimo. For another client he investigated how long it took to find a needle in a haystack (eighty-two hours). Other times he led a bull into a china shop and hired actors to dress up as turnips and donate blood, verifying that you could indeed get blood from a turnip. Long after each hooha died down, people remembered the clever idea and Moran, not the sponsors.

Showmanship can also get out of hand. P. T. Barnum, the man who said, "There's a sucker born every minute," created a magnet event when he hitched an elephant to a plow beside the train tracks to announce that his circus had come to town. He did attract newsmen and the public, but it became and remains illegal in North Carolina to plow a field with an elephant. Two generations ago, no Hollywood studio would release a movie without some wild, outrageous feat, and during the sixties, simple political theater often lured the press, but the public appears to be more sophisticated these days. Although Richard Falk still sponsors Publicity Stunt Day every year on April 1, many are now skeptical of anything that gets dubbed a "publicity stunt"—an event with no apparent substance or value beyond attracting attention.

Guidelines for a Successful Magnet Event

If you want to take on the challenge of a magnet event, keep these tips in mind.

1. *Make sure your concept is clear.* One of the reasons Take Our Daughters to Work Day succeeded, says Nell Merlino, is that the title of the event named something simple people could do to participate. If the success of your event depends on rallying participation, people must be able to "get it" from a headline, a calendar listing, a snippet on the radio.

2. *Plan far enough in advance.* Timing is critical! Find out and meet the deadlines for key event listings, public service announcements, and pre-event articles that will reach your target market.

3. *Consider enlisting the aid of cosponsors who can help spread the word.* Debbi Karpowicz proved a master at this for the swirl of events promoting her book, *I Love Men in Tasseled Loafers*. She arranged for book signings in Nordstrom's shoe department. She persuaded the Omni Hotel to host two booksigning parties where they played foot-oriented songs and gave a prize (a shoe) to the best dancer. For free, the New England Bartenders School created a new drink, The Tasseled Loafer, to be served at the parties. She got loafer tassels and brand-name shoe boxes from the Allen-Edmonds company and talked Pappagallo, a maker of women's shoes, into sending her a crate of women's shoes, from which she could choose in dressing for her publicity events.

4. *Try for triple-barreled publicity—before, during, and af-ter the event.* "Despite the best advance publicity in the world, some international leader could get assassinated and wipe ev-erything else out of the news," says Nell Merlino. "You can't help it." Right, you wouldn't have gotten TV and newspaper coverage of the event itself, but if you had some pretext for postevent publicity—say, an award given out at the event—you might still get press after the fact, in addition to before. As the song says, two out of three ain't bad.

On-Line Special Events

Bill Adler, a Washington, D. C. literary agent and book pack-ager, has pioneered a publicity event on computer networks that he calls an electronic book tour. His company posts notices to the appropriate clusters of special-interest subscribers on commercial computer networks such as America Online and CompuServe saying that next Wednesday, the author of such and such a book will be available to answer questions about a certain topic. If Jane Cullen, for example, has published a book called *Perfect Parenting*, the announcement would appear in all the so-called "forums" where people concerned with education, child care, health and safety, and parenting exchange electronic messages. The next Wednesday, a greeting from Jane introduces herself and her book and invites questions about parenting. Questions come in, and Cullen answers them and continues re-sponding to the resulting interchanges over the next few weeks until responses trail off.

"In this way we reach forty thousand to two hundred thou-sand potential book buyers in a short period of time," says Adler. "Although just a few dozen people might chime in, thou-sands of other subscribers are sitting back watching the action. The emphasis is on the information, not the book per se, but these are people passionately interested in a subject and used to buying books." During that concentrated period, this publicity method requires a lot of time to collect and respond to all the messages promptly. "You'd better have alternative computer ac-cess available in case yours crashes," Adler warns, "and you need to be prepared to go on-line twice a day. People will get mad if you've promised to answer their questions and don't do it right away."

Creative publicity hounds not in the book business can of course adapt this idea and make it more of an ongoing publicity effort than a special event. Because of the chummy atmosphere of many electronic communities, Adler cautions against barging into an established group with a blatant ad for your product or service. "Most networks have rules against commercial notices, but there's a lot of leeway in interpreting that, and the latitude goes toward people who are known. It's best to join a network and exchange messages for a month or so before mentioning what you're trying to promote. People don't like to feel like they're being sold something, but if they get to know you, they'll respect you and be kind to you. Treat the people on the network as friends even though you never actually meet. Subtlety and a helpful attitude about people's questions go a long way in spreading the word electronically."

CHAPTER 11

Speaking, for Fee or Free

In survey after survey, public speaking turns up as the number-one fear of adults—more prevalent than fear of snakes, the IRS, or death. Even professional actors and accomplished orators confess to occasional attacks of the shakes before they step out on stage. For many people, performing before others represents the ultimate vulnerability. Suppose you forget what you wanted to say? Suppose people laugh when they're not supposed to or fall asleep? Yet according to many who have mastered public speaking, acquiring comfort in front of an audience is worth the effort, since it represents the ultimate opportunity to win credibility and spread awareness of what you do.

"For selling books, speaking is much more effective than radio or TV," argues Jay Conrad Levinson, author of the "Guerrilla Marketing" series of books and an active seminar leader since 1979. "Radio and TV segments are superficial—only seven minutes long or less. But if you speak for three hours, people learn and realize that there's even more to learn, so they buy books, and tell their friends. Company owners sit there and realize they need to buy a book for each of their marketing people. Had I not been out there speaking, I'm certain that my books would have ended up on the remainder tables long ago." Instead, Levinson's 1984 book, *Guerrilla Marketing*, has spawned four sequels, two spinoffs, a software program, and a newsletter.

"Speaking is the least expensive way to promote your services," says Patricia Fripp, a former president of the National Speakers Association whom *Meetings & Conventions* magazine called "one of the ten most electrifying speakers in North America." She points out two multiplier effects that increase your impact beyond the number of people gathered in your audience. "If you speak to a group of thirty, your sign-up statistics will be much better than if you talked to thirty people one-on-one. Regardless of how good you are at what you do, by virtue of being able to stand on your feet and give a speech, you're considered more of an expert than you probably even are. In addition, you can reach out beyond the thirty people by saying at the end of the talk, 'If any of you belong to any groups that might want a speaker on my subject, please give my card to your program planner.' "

When you link media publicity and public speaking, the multiplication of impact can become exponential. This includes classes, seminars, workshops, lectures, speeches, and panel discussions for either the general public or members of an organization. In at least seven different ways, even the humblest free speaking engagement sets up the possibility of or the pretext for free media coverage.

How Speaking Produces Media Publicity

1. *A printed catalog disseminates your name and qualifications.* Teaching adult education classes of freelance writing got me started, unintentionally, in consulting. A Harvard Business School professor whom I knew slightly called and said he'd seen the notice for my course but couldn't make the date. Would I be willing to come to his office and present the class to him privately? Sure! I plucked a per-hour figure out of the air and discussed writing with him for about seven sessions. After I received a second such request, from a stranger, I realized that I could call myself a writing consultant and develop that as a

sideline to writing and speaking. Consulting now brings in about 20 percent of my income. Others I know who teach in adult education programs say they regularly get consulting inquiries traceable to appearing in the catalog. In effect, any printed catalog constitutes free publicity for your service as well as for your class.

2. *Journalists, specifically invited or not, may attend your talk.* A freelance writer who attended Barbara Winter's "Making a Living Without a Job" workshop in Minneapolis published an article about it in *Minnesota Monthly,* the magazine of the area's public radio station. "The impact on my classes was extraordinary," she says. "At the next workshop after the article appeared, I had eighty registrants, more than a third of whom came as a direct result of the article. And there's been a residual effect. For the next five years I consistently had sixty people per class, as compared with forty-five before the article came out."

3. *Reporters or producers might call after spotting a notice about your talk.* My first appearance on a radio talk show came about because a producer saw my course listing in the catalog of the Learning Connection in Providence, Rhode Island. Similarly, I called to interview Laurie Schloff for an article in *New Woman* because of her course listing in the catalog of the Boston Center for Adult Education. After that interview she asked if I'd be interesting in collaborating with her on a book, which as of this date we have actually done twice. New York City therapist Linda Barbanel never leaves the publicity potential of speaking to chance. From the very first time she spoke on the psychology of money, at her temple, she would send an announcement of her lecture or workshop to the press. The first year she was quoted in *Money* and *Savvy,* the second year in a total of nine magazines. By continually building on her previous publicity, she now receives an average of three calls per week from reporters and producers.

4. *You can initiate pre-event publicity.* In the fall of 1992, Jeanne Gavrin, a Weston, Massachusetts, therapist and nurse who specializes in treating eating disorders, arranged to present a talk on how body image affects children at St. Anne's-in-the-Fields, a church in nearby Lincoln. She sent a press release to the local papers, and a staff writer from the *Lincoln Journal* came out and interviewed her. The resulting article and photo

appeared before Gavrin's talk and, she says, got concerned parents to attend who otherwise wouldn't have come. Likewise, whenever management consultant Alan Weiss has a speaking date in, say, Dayton, Ohio, he'll send a press release to the Dayton newspaper. If it prints something, he clips it and adds it to his press kit. "When a client in Chicago sees that, they may pay more attention," he says. Don't forget to pursue free calendar listings, which may reach as many people before your talk as a feature article.

5. *You can set in motion post-event publicity.* After your speaking engagement, send a notice or press release to your alumni magazine, your hometown newspaper, and the newsletters of local or national organizations you belong to.

6. *The sponsor of your presentation can recommend you to the media or directly to clients.* Journalists and clients regard an organization that sponsors talks and seminars as a referral resource. Jay Levinson, who teaches through the University of California's community education system, says that when large organizations seek a presenter, they tend to contact universities first, rather than speaking agents, for recommendations. "A univerity has so much credibility, even though you don't need academic qualifications to teach in the extension program," Levinson says. By forming a relationship with such an educational organization, you have someone primed to pass the word about you at no cost to you.

7. *The sponsor of your presentation can publicize you in its own media.* Get copies of an organization's flyers or press releases announcing your talk and any pre-event and post-event publicity in its newsletter. When Alan Weiss presented a keynote speech to the Inland Press Association, the group produced an attractive 8-½″ × 11″ flyer with excerpts from Weiss's writings on the reverse. He secured permission to reprint it for his press kit. Since the flyer includes the organization's logo, it's more impressive than something Weiss could produce on his own. Here the coup to top all coups is persuading a media entity to sponsor your seminar. Phillip Rierdan of Executive Briefing Sessions in Framingham, Massachusetts, has as cosponsors of his seminar, "How to Bring in New Business," WRKO, a talk radio station, and *Boston Business Journal*, both of which run free

advertisements for him to hundreds of thousands of listeners and readers.

Want to Speak? Let's Count the Ways

The terminology of speaking is somewhat fluid, with some people saying "workshop" for what other people call a "seminar," "presentation," or "class." So don't get hung up on what to call different kinds of speaking engagements. Instead, first think strategically about sponsorship.

• *Self-sponsored public seminars and talks.* If you have to hire a hotel meeting room and send out flyers to a mailing list, this option is risky. Regardless of what you may have heard about typical response rates, dramatic public seminar flops happen all the time. In 1982 Paul and Sarah Edwards launched a seminar on the topic that has since made them famous—"How to Start a Home-Based Business." They rented hotel rooms and ran ads in major newspapers. In Sacramento, however, not one person enrolled, and in San Jose only eight to ten people showed up. "We were ahead of the market, and we lost thousands of dollars—a lot of money for us at that time," Paul Edwards recalls. In connection with public seminars, send press releases to the media and invite reporters to attend as your guests.

• *Sponsored public presentations.* Sponsors range from adult education programs to nonprofit organizations, such as libraries, museums, churches, or interest groups such as the Historic Preservation Society or Pollution Control Advocates United. Professional or civic organizations that open their meetings to the public would fall under this category as well, as would for-profit businesses that sponsor lectures, such as bookstores. Usually the sponsoring organization routinely takes care of publicity, but you should feel free to write your own lively press release or, for an out-of-the-ordinary talk, try phone pitches to key columnists and reporters.

If you have never taught in an adult education program, I urge you to consider it. Although high school, college, or university extension programs and independent adult education centers usually pay teachers only a small honorarium, their catalogs reach tens or hundreds of thousands of people. I know consultants and lawyers who normally charge $90 an hour or more who find the exposure valuable enough to continue to teach in these programs for one-fifth that amount. Adult education also represents an opportunity to gain confidence in your expertise in an informal classroom setting before a small, interested group. Programming personnel provide expert advice on your catalog copy, dates and times, and a free testing ground for new programs. On the other hand, because of a case in Florida where both an investment advisor and the institution that sponsored his class were sued for unethical influence on students, many adult education programs have strict guidelines controlling teachers' marketing, including distribution of business cards or brochures, at their classes.

To propose an adult education class, examine the program's current list of offerings and write a title and one-paragraph description that doesn't duplicate what they already have. Add a brief summary of your qualifications to teach the class and send it to the program director. To get maximum exposure with minimal time commitment, follow my policy of doing several one-shot programs at different locations, rather than four-to-ten-week courses.

• *Sponsored organizational presentations.* These talks are publicized primarily to members of the sponsoring group, such as a Chamber of Commerce, Kiwanis Club, Valley Bar Association, or State Culinary Arts Society. Local lunch or dinner meetings on what is semiaffectionately dubbed the "Rubber Chicken Circuit" do not usually pay speakers, but many regional or national conferences do. Peruse the *Encyclopedia of Associations* (see Chapter 23) or the Yellow Pages under "Associations" to locate prospect groups and contact the program chairperson, who will often be thrilled to hear from you. You can stretch the pre-event appeal and post-event impact of your talk to members not present by contributing an article to the organization's newsletter.

Large conferences commonly include the audiotaping of all sessions for the benefit of nonattendees and attendees who couldn't attend all sessions. They'll usually let you have or at least borrow the master tape for your session so that you can make copies to sell or use to prove your speaking prowess to other sponsoring groups. Although many organizations routinely slap their copyright on such tapes, insist on retaining copyright to your presentation or you may encounter problems later on if you try to fashion your expertise into a book.

• *In-house talks.* When a company engages your speaking services for its employees, you will almost always be paid, sometimes quite handsomely. Except for an endorsement or a notice in the company newsletter, however, these gigs have little publicity potential.

The Talk Itself

Let's say you've volunteered to be the luncheon speaker at your chapter of the Lions Club, your first time speaking before a group since you blundered through an oral report in college. Patricia Fripp suggests keeping your presentation simple, calling upon skills you exercise all the time. "If you just stand up and say, 'The five questions I'm most frequently asked about ———— (whatever you do) are . . .' and then answer those questions conversationally, that's a speech," Fripp says. "You've probably answered those questions dozens of times at cocktail parties, and the people you're speaking to are just like the people you meet at parties." As you gain experience and speak on more formal occasions, use these tips to keep audiences awake and involved.

1. *Plan your talk using a simple four-part formula.* You may have heard the advice, "Tell 'em what you're going to tell 'em, tell 'em, then tell 'em what you told 'em," but I think a slightly different schema works better. First hook the audience's interest with a brief story, a set of questions that elicit a show of hands or startling statistics. Then state the focus of the talk and any background or practical details needed to orient the audience. Next present your content. Finally, pull things together with a closing story, a restatement of your main theme, or an appeal to action.

2. *Customize your remarks for your audience.* No audience likes a "If this is Tuesday, are you the dentists?" attitude in a speaker. Listeners relax and like you more when you weave in words, examples, and names relevant to their industry, locality, and occupational concerns. But take special care with names and terms unfamiliar to you. I'll never forget the time a conference speaker offered praise of the organization's president, but pronounced his name wrong. You could almost hear a collective "ouch!" in the room. As you speak in different places and for different groups, you'll notice that reactions to the same material may vary radically. I have a story about how I got started in writing that elicits out-loud laughs in Cambridge, just a few smiles across the river in Boston, and mostly blank looks in the hinterlands. I've also observed that while working adults enjoy the real-world flavor of personal anecdotes, college students tend to find them egotistical and irrelevant.

3. *When possible, include some form of audience participation.* Studies show that when people participate in a presentation, the material becomes at least three times more memorable than if they merely listen to a lecture. With a small group, it's easier to encourage and manage comments and questions from the audience, but some forms of participation work even with a group in the hundreds. If your microphone arrangement allows, you can move off the podium and interact with individuals in the audience like Donahue or Oprah. Fill-in-the-blank handouts, on which you provide the basic structure of your talk and leave blanks sprinkled throughout your list of the key points, keep an audience involved throughout an information-rich speech. Even asking rhetorical questions ("Can you remember what motivated *you* to go into accounting?") helps—people answer in their own minds before you go on. In any group larger than twenty or twenty-five, remember to repeat audience questions for the whole assemblage.

4. *Practice your talk out loud, either for a friend or in front of a mirror.* Just as familiarizing yourself with a musical score wouldn't necessarily get your fingers doing the right thing at the piano, having a great outline and good notes for a talk doesn't ensure a smooth performance. Actually saying the words in proper sequence helps immeasurably more.

5. *Don't get hung up on fancy visuals.* Although some circles

expect slick slides, overheads, or other visual aids, use them only to the extent that they clarify information that would otherwise be difficult to absorb. Jay Levinson confesses that he hired LucasFilm to make up slides for his seminars but soon put those slides permanently away. "They were beautiful, but people were always so busy taking notes they didn't have a chance to look up," he explains. "Besides, I never say the same thing twice." If you're a spellbinding storyteller, but would panic if a bulb burned out, or can never remember which button to press on the slide clicker, follow Levinson's lead and go solo up there.

6. *Know how to channel nervousness.* Expect some jitters and do your best anyway. In *Smart Speaking* (see Chapter 23), Laurie Schloff and I describe several easy ways to keep nervousness under control. With the "Pick-a-Tic" technique, for example, you choose how your body expresses the terror you feel. Out of the audience's line of sight, simply press your thumb and middle finger together for three seconds and slowly let go. Or interpret—"reframe," some psychologists call it—any physical symptoms in a positive, productive way: "I'm feeling excited because I'm eager to do a good job, and I will."

7. *Keep within your allotted time.* Break this rule and you'll find word of mouth running heavily against you.

Advanced Tactics for Ensuring That Speaking Pays Off

• *Write your own introduction.* Every experienced speaker has a story about the person delegated to introduce him or her to a group who babbled irrelevantly, said something false, or even inflicted a mild insult. The solution: Type out exactly what you'd like the introducer to say on an index card and request that those few sentences be delivered word for word.

• *Design your own evaluation forms.* Many organizations have either no evaluation forms or one that provides no useful information. See Chapter 19 on some questions that do better than others at eliciting usable blurbs. If the organization distributes evaluation forms that include numerical scales, don't attach much importance to the fact that you achieved an average rating of only 3.9 out of 5, or an average of "very good" rather than "excellent." In my experience, such ratings are heavily influenced by the time of day, participants' expectations, and other factors beyond your control. The pattern of substantive comments tends to be much more revealing.

• *Try to get a list of those present at your talks.* Do this even if you don't yet know what you would do with a mailing list. By the time you have a reason to recontact people who have heard you speak, you'll already be on your way to a substantial customer database. At a small to midsized class or workshop, send around a pad headed with "Name and address if you'd like to be on Sara Speaker's mailing list." For a sponsored talk, some organizations routinely present speakers with a participant list, while with other sponsors you need more creative tactics. Ask people to bring their business cards to you or your product table after the talk, for instance, to be eligible for a raffled prize.

• *Mention your services or special features of your business casually within your talk.* "No one really hears your bio when you're introduced," says Claudyne Wilder, who among other activities conducts presentation skills seminars that demonstrate Polaroid's LCD panel technology. "Allude to your expertise in the middle of your talk. They'll hear it more." To mention it naturally and without veering off into a sales pitch, simply work in occasional phrases like, "As often happens when I help clients plan for their kids' college education . . . ," or "Somebody who came to one of our Saturday morning computer workshops for kids said . . ." The more concrete, specific, and fleeting these references are, the better.

• *Survey audiences.* If the setup permits, invite audience members to fill out a survey or questionnaire. From one large group or several smaller groups, you can collect newsworthy data that merits media publicity. (See Chapter 2.)

• *Cultivate your speaking skills through private coaching, the National Speakers Association, or Toastmasters* (see Chapter 23 for contact information). If you discover that you enjoy speaking, with professional feedback and exposure to master presenters you'll learn how to deserve and command higher fees. Patricia Fripp started out as a hairdresser who addressed Rotary Clubs and other civic groups on motivational topics. At the suggestion of a friend, she attended a conference of the National Speakers Association, where she delivered fifteen minutes of her motivational spiel and was "discovered" by an agent. "Wow," she said to herself as she soon faced an audience of 2,000 for the first time. "For this I could give up cutting hair." Through hard work and constant practice, she developed her skills to the point where she could quit the hair salon and earn thousands of dollars per keynote speech.

• *Once you're successful, investigate agents.* Like literary agents, speaking agents and bureaus are rarely interested in representing you until you're already consistently earning fees that would mean significant commissions for them. In fact, "representing you" is somewhat misleading, since their mission is to supply organizations with appropriate talent—not to market each and every speaker in their stable. Yet good bureaus and agents are extremely well networked with corporations and associations that regularly hire speakers and can help you secure lucrative bookings. For partial listings of lecture bureaus and speaking agents, consult *Literary Market Place* or Jeffrey Lant's *The Unabashed Self-Promoter's Guide.*

Jay Levinson bypasses the bureaus with a speaking agent who acts more like a personal promoter, marketing Levinson's seminars aggressively and exclusively. "He's an angel from heaven," says Levinson of Bill Shear, who handles all the arrangements for Levinson's optimal quota of three appearances a month. So grateful is the "Guerrilla Marketing" guru for the carefree boost Shear's work has given his career that he not only pays Shear the standard commission for seminar bookings but also, voluntarily, 10 percent of the royalties from all of his books.

CHAPTER 12

Hitting the Airwaves, on Radio or TV

Mention "TV" or "radio" in the context of free publicity and most people's minds lock onto being a guest on an interview show. But the airwaves actually hold a much wider band of opportunities for the publicity hound. While *Donahue* or *Geraldo* may expose you to the broadest daytime national TV audience, some of the other options offer a more consistent, targeted impact and more control.

In Macon, Georgia, for example, psychologist Amy Flowers has a regular ninety-second spot called "Creative Coping" on radio station WPEZ (Z108). Every Monday, Tuesday, and Wednesday, her voice comes on the air just before noon and talks to listeners about common mental health problems such as handling stress or being more assertive. Starting with a teaser, such as "Does your mother ever make you crazy?" she defines a problem, provides perspective on it, and supplies solutions, all in an optimistic, friendly, jargon-free tone. "I love doing it," says Flowers, who collects ideas from magazines, Ann Landers, and conversations in and out of her office. Recently, a woman driving through Macon heard the spot and called for an appointment even though she lives forty-five miles away from Focal Pointe

Women, the clinic where Flowers practices. In the five years "Creative Coping" has been on the air, seventy-five people have ordered free transcripts. Yet Flowers is even more excited about another kind of response to her spot. "It gives me a chance to ethically educate people and to destigmatize therapy, so that people who need help aren't afraid to come in. If they hear me on the radio and that takes the fear out of counseling, then I've accomplished my purpose."

Flowers feels much more in tune with radio than TV. "I've been on TV five or six times, and I'm still uncomfortable with it. I'm conscious that people are looking at me, and I have to be clever besides." Not only is "Creative Coping" scripted, eliminating the pressure for snappy ad-libbing, the technician in the studio where she records it can edit any rough spots. She has also been careful to retain the copyright on her material so that she can take her spot beyond Georgia in the future.

The format Amy Flowers uses can work for almost any expert, whether your field is cars, country living, or creativity. But additional options for exposure on the air abound, some of which are almost as accessible as an old-fashioned soapbox.

The Most Accessible Opportunity of All

Some media critics like to say that freedom of the press belongs to those who own the presses, but in the case of public-access cable TV, you as Joe or Jane Public in effect own the medium. To receive a license that gives them a monopoly to provide cable service for a certain locality, cable companies must provide a channel open to any qualified person or group in that locality who wishes to air a program. Here "qualified" means "technically qualified," and cable companies must also provide training so that those who wish to can learn to produce their own programs. According to Geri Michael Hackel, who produces a news show for the Boston public-access station, the free training, which at her station takes ten to twelve weeks, can be worth thousands of dollars. Beyond requiring that you have technical competence and that you live or have a business in the subscription area of the station, these stations are not allowed to impose any other qualifications. Whether you want to sermonize about the right of companies to pollute the environment, present your off-color comedy act, or interview all your law partners about their areas of expertise, they must allow you on the air when your turn comes up.

Unlike broadcast TV or radio, your potential viewing audience is limited to cable subscribers in a strictly delimited area, usually your town or city. In a metropolis like Boston, that adds up to a significant opportunity, especially if you will be offering something likely to build a regular audience or catch the attention of channel cruisers. In a smaller area, a public-access cable show gives you excellent exposure if your primary target market is local. If you'd like to reach a regional or national audience, this medium still might be worthwhile: You'll get precious practice and can try to interest other areas in using tapes of your show.

As Valla Dana Fotiades discovered in the first year and a half that she produced her interview show, *Valla & . . .* , in Worcester, Massachusetts, other benefits can trickle in from a regular cable program. "I'm just launching my speaking career, and having my own show gives me an opportunity to make easy cold calls, inviting people on my program. I help them, and it has come back in speaking business for me. Also, two consultants I had on the show asked for a copy of the tape, which they are sending to their clients and prospects around the world."

On the other hand, stations don't furnish a crew to shoot your show. While they may give you a list of volunteers, it's up to you to spark enthusiasm, commitment, and quality in at least three and preferably five or more technically qualified people each time you shoot a show. Some of the help needed, such as graphics, is simple enough that Fotiades has been able to use her thirteen-year-old son and her director's eleven-year-old daughter as part of the crew. Bill Costley, who lives in the 6,000-subscriber town of Wellesley, Massachusetts, streamlined his crew for *Author!*, a twelve-part interview series on writers with Wellesley connections. He got by with a crew of three: the interviewer (and coproducer), the studio manager (and director), and himself on two cameras, one stationary, as floor manager and coproducer. Shoots never had to be cancelled for lack of volunteers. A local author himself, Costley deliberately remained off-camera in the series. "If you try to glorify yourself, crews and audiences gradually drift away," he says. "Those who crave stardom should seek it somewhere else." Costley's nonstarring participation in community-access TV, dating back to 1986, had previously led to a front-page feature story in the *Wellesley Townsman*.

Since Costley's *Author!* series had archival value for his town and wider appeal, he donated a videocassette of the programs to the Wellesley library's audiovisual department, which circulates it among a computerized network of twenty-two public and two academic libraries along Route 128, west and north of Boston. "Despite budgetary problems, public libraries are busily expanding their electronic holdings," he says. Valla Dana Fotiades adds that tapes from Worcester sometimes "bicycle" around to stations in four smaller Massachusetts towns before returning to Worcester. Create connections with big-city stations, she suggests, and you could exchange your way to a major impact on cable.

If public-access programming seems to you like a good launchpad for publicity, just call the cable company that serves your locality and find out when the next training course begins.

Being an Interview Guest

Participating in someone else's interview show takes much less work than producing your own. When the show has a large audience, the payoff can be huge. Publishing analyst John Kremer says that one appearance on *Oprah!*, when Oprah expresses enthusiasm for a guest's book, can sell 50,000 copies. "If you're up there with nine other people, though, it may not do much," he says. Yet everyone I've spoken with who's appeared on one of the major interview shows reports that their prestige skyrocketed. For this reason, Jeff Slutsky, who calls his experience with the Sally Jessy Raphael show "horrendous," nevertheless says he'd do it again in a minute. "When people look at my bio, they don't know it was a lousy show," he says. The cumulative effect of many smaller shows can be significant as well.

Within the category of interview shows, formats differ. Sometimes for TV you'll sit with the host in a fake living room and trade pleasant, mildly informative banter. Other times a studio audience participates in the show with questions and comments. You may be on alone or with a long lineup of guests. Both radio and TV shows may include anonymous callers who sound off, ask for information, or try to put you on the spot. For radio, you may do the show either in the station's studio or by telephone from your home or office. Any show can be either live or taped.

Think about which kind of show seems best for you and which medium, radio or TV, you prefer. Therapist Szifra Birke worries much more in connection with TV. "I get caught up with what image I want to put across—casual Cambridge, sporty sophisticate, or power broker." Social worker Merle Bombardieri finds call-in shows fun because she gets a sense of the audience but risky because callers can get the show off track. "On TV people get to meet me, not just my voice," adds Bombardieri. "I like that." Therapist Linda Barbanel likes *Good Day New York* best because it positions her as a featured expert who explains the taped man-in-the-street comments on the issue of the day. Many shows put more emphasis on the testimony and emotions of the guests.

As I discussed in Chapter 4, your library probably carries some of the media directories that contain contact names, addresses, and phone numbers of radio and TV shows across the United States. Ask your reference librarian about a media guide for your city or state, or consult these works:

- *Working Press of the Nation*, Volume 3
- *Gale Directory of Publications & Broadcast Media*
- *Bacon's Radio/TV Directory*
- *Broadcasting & Cable Yearbook*

For any shows you especially hope to get on, it's prudent to call and confirm the names and spelling of the person who should receive your information.

Once you've selected a show or shows to target and learned the name of the producer, try one of the three approaches to becoming an interview subject: Make a phone pitch, being especially conscious that you may be interrupting someone working on deadline (see Chapter 16). Or write a pitch letter, explaining what you'd be able to discuss and how it would benefit listeners or viewers (see Chapter 6). Or send a press release, either alone or accompanied by your press kit (see Chapter 5). According to broadcast media maven Larry Rochester, many talk-show producers look down their noses at potential guests calling on their own behalf. So for this purpose alone you may want to enlist a friend, relative, or employee to call on your behalf. Whoever calls must be enthusiastic, clear, concise, and prepared to elicit and keep track of many nitty-gritty details about the show in case the pitch wins a "yes." After your first "yes" read Chapter 15 especially carefully, so that you make the most of being a guest on the airwaves.

Appearing on the News

Although much of radio and TV news focuses on governmental and political developments, it includes coverage of business, scientific, and entertainment innovations, profiles of community problem-solvers, and stories about special events—indeed, most of the topics you'd find in the newspaper. You'll do best on radio and TV news with either a happening-right-here-this-very-week hook or what media people call an "evergreen" topic, where there's no more reason to run it this week than last week, last month, or even last year. Timeless topics such as what to do about varicose veins come in handy when a station has several gaping minutes to fill on a slow news day. I remember a piece at the very end of the evening news on one of the networks about a professor who runs a grammar hotline, where he gives authoritative answers to callers asking, say, about "like" versus "as," or whether "impact" should be used as a verb. By cutting back and forth from the reporter's statements, filled with typical mistakes, to the professor's good-humored, pedantic corrections, the reporter made an undramatic topic thoroughly charming, to a writer at least. I don't remember, however, the professor's name or what college he taught at, much less his hotline number, which embodies the weakness of broadcast news as compared with print. From a newspaper I'd have that information in black and white.

While some organizations plant themselves on TV by spending tens of thousands of dollars on video news releases—
prepackaged features that include a very subtle sell—you can
match their success with nothing more than shrewd thinking
and good communication skills. Either through a pitch letter, a
press release, or a phone call, stress the timeliness, the visual
(for TV) or auditory (for radio) drama of your hook, and the importance for listeners or viewers. Lila Ivey, former producer of
the 5:00 news on WLNE in Providence, Rhode Island, recalls a
pitch that won her over because it met all three of those tests.
"A publicist from the University of Rhode Island told me how
colorful their jellyfish tanks were, that July was jellyfish month,
and that it was important to tell beachgoers which jellyfish to
watch out for, which ones sting." Bill Costley, who serves as
publicist for the Wellesley Symphony Orchestra in Massachusetts, says that he usually beats out other organizations compet-
ing for airtime to tell listeners on WBZ Radio about upcoming
events by sending stories with more depth and timeliness than
the average event announcement. For a concert featuring the
composers Dvorak and Tchaikovsky, for instance, he tied the
program to the recent political turmoil in Czechoslovakia and
Russia.

If a radio or TV station does send a crew to you to prepare
a news story, some guidelines apply in addition to those discussed in Chapters 14 and 15. "Never call and cancel," advises
Lila Ivey. "If you do, you've burned your bridges for a long, long
time. If an emergency comes up, get someone to fill in. Have a
backup plan." Fax clear, accurate directions to find you, and
when the crew arrives, have two people, not one or five, available for interviews. Feel free to make suggestions, "but don't tell
me how to do my job," warns Ivey. "We're not MGM Studios. I
know what we can do and still get on the air at five o'clock."
The worst and most common blunder, she says, is grabbing the
microphone. Assume that the technicians know more about
what they're doing than you do. Finally, if a crew arrives and
then rushes off because a big fire breaks out, "Don't whine.
They'll try to get back to you."

To get onto news programs in a more consistent and controlled fashion, consider proposing a regular spot, like Amy
Flowers's "Creative Coping." Lila Ivey's former station, Channel

6 in Providence, has local movie reviewers, a nutritionist, a chef, and a master gardener who appear weekly at a regular time for two minutes. Ivey says that credentials count most in a potential regular, then whether or not they can write their own material and have a personality that can come across well on TV. If this option grabs you, research which station in your area might be receptive to your idea, call the receptionist to find out who to send your proposal to, and write a captivating query letter, similar to the sample in Chapter 8, detailing your concept and your qualifications. Just as with a newspaper column (see Chapter 9), you have a good chance of a station running your segment for free if you design it to be informational, entertaining and meeting viewer or listener needs.

Other Publicity Opportunities on Radio or TV

1. *Public service announcements (PSAs)*. Most radio stations and many TV stations air announcements of events of interest to their audience that are sponsored by nonprofit organizations. Follow the format of the sample below, which Bob Piankian of Boston wrote and sent to the local classical music stations. Use all capitals, with reading time indicated. For TV, it's worthwhile to send along a prop, like a customized mug or T-shirt, that the station can hold up while making the announcement.

Sample Public Service Announcement

Press Contact: Bob Piankian
(617) 254–3088

<u>FOR IMMEDIATE RELEASE</u>
<u>MAY 16, 1993</u>

<u>KILL DATE: JUNE 5, 1993</u>

<u>METROPOLITAN WIND SYMPHONY HOSTS 5TH ANNUAL</u>
<u>BOSTON FESTIVAL OF BANDS</u>
PUBLIC SERVICE ANNOUNCEMENT/COMMUNITY CALENDAR

15 SECOND: THE METROPOLITAN WIND SYMPHONY HOSTS THE FIFTH ANNUAL BOSTON FESTIVAL OF BANDS ON SATURDAY JUNE 5 FROM 10 AM TO 6 PM AT FANEUIL HALL, ADJACENT TO QUINCY MARKETPLACE IN BOSTON. EIGHT BANDS WILL PLAY A WIDE VARIETY OF MUSIC. ADMISSION IS FREE. FOR INFORMATION CALL (617) 522–2849.

20 SECOND: THE METROPOLITAN WIND SYMPHONY HOSTS THE FIFTH ANNUAL BOSTON FESTIVAL OF BANDS ON SATURDAY JUNE 5 FROM 10 AM TO 6 PM AT FANEUIL HALL, ADJACENT TO QUINCY MARKETPLACE IN BOSTON. OTHER BANDS PERFORMING INCLUDE THE AIR FORCE BAND OF LIBERTY, THE AMERICAN BAND, AND THE CONCORD BAND. THE BANDS WILL PLAY SELECTIONS RANGING FROM BROADWAY SHOW MUSIC TO SOUSA MARCHES TO CLAS-SICAL MUSIC. ADMISSION IS FREE. FOR MORE INFORMATION CALL (617) 522–2849.

45 SECOND: THE METROPOLITAN WIND SYMPHONY HOSTS

THE FIFTH ANNUAL BOSTON FESTIVAL OF BANDS ON SATURDAY JUNE 5 FROM 10 AM TO 6 PM AT FANEUIL HALL, ADJACENT TO QUINCY MARKETPLACE IN BOSTON. OTHER BANDS PERFORMING INCLUDE THE AIR FORCE BAND OF LIBERTY, THE AMERICAN BAND, THE METROWEST BAND, THE STRAFFORD COUNTY WIND SYMPHONY, THE NEW ENGLAND BRASS BAND, THE CASCO BAY CONCERT BAND, AND THE CONCORD BAND. MUSIC DIRECTOR DAVID MARTINS OF THE UNIVERSITY OF LOWELL DIRECTS THE MWS. THE BANDS WILL PLAY SELECTIONS RANGING FROM BROADWAY SHOW MUSIC TO SOUSA MARCHES TO CLASSICAL MUSIC. RADIO STATION WCRB IS COSPONSORING THE EVENT AND PETER ROSS OF WCRB WILL ANNOUNCE IT. ADMISSION IS FREE.

THE CONCERT IS WHEELCHAIR-ACCESSIBLE. TO GET MORE INFORMATION CALL THE MWS CONCERT LINE AT (617) 522-2849. A PART OF BOSTON'S MUSICAL COMMUNITY SINCE 1971, THE MWS IS A NONPROFIT SEMI-PROFESSIONAL ENSEMBLE COMPRISED OF APPROXIMATELY 70 TALENTED MUSICIANS FROM THE GREATER BOSTON METROPOLITAN AREA.

2. *Editorial replies.* Another opportunity especially open to nonprofit groups is free air time to respond to a station-sponsored editorial that presented only one side of an issue. The federal Fairness Doctrine mandates that stations provide balanced coverage, so if the station does not respond reasonably to your request, you may appeal to the Federal Communications Commission (FCC). If you can make a case that a feature show, documentary, or news item constituted unbalanced coverage, you may have the same right of reply. Call the offending station and find out to whom you should send your letter requesting reply time. In your letter, be as specific as possible about what was unfair and why and how you propose to remedy the lack of balance.

3. *Bulletin boards.* Some commercial and noncommercial TV

stations that do not broadcast twenty-four hours a day fill their screens with rotating community announcements during off hours. Again, contact the station to find out its guidelines.

4. *College radio and TV stations.* Some college stations open the airwaves to local people unaffiliated with the college. On Wellesley College's WZLY-FM, students get first choice of time slots, Wellesley residents next, and finally others living in the ten-mile listening radius. From 1983 to 1988 Bill Costley did arts interviews live on the station in a slot no one else wanted— Sunday mornings following the broadcast of a local church service for shut-ins. "Since the service ended anywhere from eleven o'clock to eleven forty-five and the next program started at noon, I had to be adaptable," he remembers. "But church listeners stayed tuned, and I developed a regular audience who recognized my voice years after the program went off the air."

5. *Commentary on National Public Radio.* All Things Considered, the evening news show on National Public Radio, regularly airs taped essay segments that offer personal and observational commentary from people who are not public figures and may live anywhere in the United States. Call the station, based in Washington, D.C., to find out who considers commentary submissions, then send both a transcript and a tape of a one-minute segment. Since the purpose of the tape is to hear how you sound, don't worry about its technical quality. If the producers like your piece, they'll arrange for you to rerecord it professionally.

6. *Game shows.* Many game-show hosts introduce contestants to viewers by the whole name, occupation, and hometown. On a show like *Jeopardy!* the host often gets contestants talking a bit about their work or hobbies. Don't pursue this avenue, though, unless you believe a particular show is consistent with your image.

7. *Exposé shows. 60 Minutes,* one of the longest-running shows on television, has spawned numerous imitators, where a reporter and camera crew pursue allegations about individuals, businesses, or organizations. It's hard to come off well if they choose you as a subject. Unless you enjoy swimming in piranha tanks, I'd stay away from shows of this sort.

8. *Your own show.* Who says you can't create your own show for commercial radio or TV? It's a traditional ploy for officeless

politicians who hope to remain visible to the public between elections. The guidelines earlier in this chapter on getting a regular spot on the news apply, but because you'd be on the air for thirty minutes at a time or more, you'll need a good deal of performance polish and, usually, broadcast experience to pull this off.

CHAPTER 13

Schmoozing That Puts You in the Public Eye

Anne Boe of Encinitas, California, takes the idea of being her own best press agent further than most. Everywhere she goes—meetings, airports, parties—she introduces herself to strangers and invites them to do the same. As a way of creating unpredictable opportunities, it works. During one speaking engagement in Washington, D. C., she left the banquet to get something from her room upstairs and found herself in an elevator with a man she'd never met. "I wasn't going to waste ten floors," she remembers, "so very quickly I said my usual, 'Hi, I'm Anne Boe. I do career management and networking. What do you do?' The man saw my speaker badge and said, 'I'm not a speaker. I write about speakers.' He worked for the magazine of Meeting Planners International and invited me to send my press kit and demo video, which I did. Six months later I spoke to his group in Phoenix and a year later was asked to keynote their conference, a real plum for speakers." The man in the elevator wasn't wearing a name tag and could have been a tourist from Walla Walla, but Boe wouldn't have gotten discouraged if he was. "Everything in life is an opportunity, yet I don't see many other people reaching out the way I do."

In her book, *Is Your "Net" Working?*, Boe discusses the art of making and keeping connections with people. Since for many people the word "networking" has taken on a shallow, opportunistic connotation, I'll talk instead about "schmoozing"—ways of cozying up to people that can pay off in publicity, even if starting a conversation in an elevator strikes you as a horrendous ordeal.

Strategic Self-Introductions

Speaking with strangers sometimes leads to spectacular results. John Kremer tells a story about one author traveling by plane who talked to her seatmate about the guidebook she'd written for handicapped travelers. The seatmate was none other than Abigail Van Buren, and after "Dear Abby" mentioned the guidebook in her syndicated column, more than two mail sacks full of orders for the guidebook materialized. I'm sure the author was glad she hadn't spent the flight with her nose buried in a novel.

But whether or not you make the first move, it's essential to have handy a quick, comprehensive, and comprehensible way of introducing yourself. How can people help spread the word about you if you say just your name, or the fact that you live in Kalamazoo or work in computers? Steve Schiffman does it this way: "I'm president of DEI Management, a sales training firm in New York City. We do a lot of business with companies like IBM and Pitney Bowes." Schiffman says he uses this self-introduction everywhere. "It can be as obnoxious as hell," he admits, "but the reality is that everyone knows someone, and it cascades."

Some schmoozing specialists take the art of strategic self-introductions one step further by recommending that instead of using an occupational title, you use your six seconds to present the benefits you or your organization produce for people. For instance, instead of saying that you're a CPA, you can say, "I specialize in helping people dramatically reduce their tax bill." Instead of saying, "I'm Vice-President of the Earthwise Foundation," you might say, "I work for an organization that helps local communities throughout the country carry out curbside recycling programs." Doesn't that grab you more? The real test, Jeff Slutsky explains in his book, *How to Get Clients*, is rattling off your carefully honed self-introduction at a cocktail party. If you've done it right, people will lean forward and ask, "No kidding! How do you do that?"—inviting you to say more.

San Franciscan Patricia Fripp says it's a great conversation starter when she's asked what she does and replies, "I make meetings and conventions more exciting." Usually that provokes another question, to which she replies, "You know how meetings are supposed to be dynamic and exciting and they're usually dull and boring? I have some practical ideas I present in an entertaining way, with the result that people stay awake, have a good time, and get the company's message. I'm a professional speaker." Fripp says this approach works especially well by making what she does for a living meaningful even to the eight out of ten people who have no idea professional speakers exist. It works just as well, she says, if you do something more familiar, like sell real estate, because it implants the idea that you can solve problems more creatively than competitors who merely say, "I'm a Realtor."

Those who are on the shy side can cut down on fear flutters by circulating at parties or business gatherings with a friend. Patricia Fripp often attends meetings with Susan RoAne, author of *How to Work a Room* and *The Secrets of Savvy Networking*. "When we meet someone, Susan will say, 'This is Patricia Fripp. She truly is one of the best speakers in the country,' and I will say, 'What Susan is too modest to tell you is that she's a bestselling author.' We act like each other's press agents." Not only is it easier to tout a friend than yourself, consider how much better an impression each of the duo makes than if Fripp said, "I'm one of the best speakers in the country," and RoAne said, "I'm a bestselling author."

Gerontologist Ruth Jacobs of Wellesley, Massachusetts, has found a way of introducing herself and inviting curious questions before she even opens her mouth. She often wears customized T-shirts that bear the legend R. A. S. P.: REMARKABLE AGING SMART PERSON or OUTRAGEOUS OLDER WOMAN. Both relate to her book, *Be an Outrageous Older Woman*, and the purple version of OUTRAGEOUS OLDER WOMAN especially attracts a lot of attention. "People come up to me and want to know where I got the T-shirt. I hand them a flyer for the book, and when they call the eight-hundred number of my publisher they usually order the T-shirt *and* the book." She also has buttons with both slogans and wears those when she's going around town on errands. "Sometimes in the supermarket someone will come up to me and get so excited about the button that I have to give it away on the spot," Jacobs says. When she speaks at conferences, a display of the buttons often draws people to the book table who end up buying the book.

Being Memorable

Besides meeting people and talking with them, artful schmoozing involves making yourself more memorable than happens in the average encounter. A catchy business name helps accomplish this. Professional organizer Cheryl Norris of Washington, D. C., calls her business name, Order Out of Chaos, "a tremendous asset." If you counted yourself among the desperately disorganized, just hearing that business name would make you prick up your ears and remember what you heard. Similarly, "Nancy Friedman, The Telephone Doctor," is more likely to stick in your mind than "Nancy Friedman, consultant on telephone skills." Another telephone skills trainer, Stan Billue, goes by the nickname "Mr. Fantastic" because of his standing offer that if you ask him how he is and he doesn't say "I'm fantastic," he will give you a hundred-dollar bill. (In the sixteen years that he's told this to hundreds of thousands of people, he's had to pay up exactly four times.) Entertainer Ron Bianco feels strongly that the name he gave his singing dog makes a difference in the response to his act. "Bilbo" has a ring to it that, for example, "Rover" does not, he says.

You might think that your personal name is not within your control the way your business name and the name of your pet are, but some disagree. Don't you find "Kirk Douglas" easier to remember (and spell) than "Issur Danielovitch," the name the actor was born with? Outside of Hollywood, the public radio star and bestselling author of *Lake Wobegon Days* goes by Garrison Keillor, but he was born with the less distinctive first name of Gary. You may not want to tamper with the name your parents gave you, but you still have choices. If your passport reads "Margaret Fox Vigilioni," are you going to go by all three names, by "Margaret Viglioni," "Margaret F. Viglioni," "Meg Viglioni," "M. Fox Viglioni," or "M. F. Viglioni"? I believe that if you want people to remember your name and cite it accurately, a middle initial is an encumbrance rather than an asset. Most ordinary people and many reporters will drop it out and you'll have an inconsistency in your press clips. If you've already become well-known by a certain name, however, whatever its flaws, stick with it.

Your appearance might form a part of your strategy of becoming unforgettable. Patricia Fripp nearly always wears a hat when she attends business meetings. "I have about seventy hats and let's just say they're very memorable," she says. "People race over to me when they see my hat and say, 'Hi, Patricia, I knew it had to be you.'" Although Fripp argues that women have an advantage in being able to dress with pizzazz, a man can stand out by always wearing a bow tie, elegant suits, or, in some careers, an unusual hairstyle. If you met boxing promoter Don King, with his electric, stand-up-by-itself hairdo, wouldn't you remember him?

Or what makes you stand out in people's memories might be your opinions. Rick Segel, owner of Ruth's, a dress shop in Medford, Massachusetts, appeared on the Sally Jessy Raphael show because of a referral from someone he hadn't spoken with in three years. The show concerned people who wear clothing and then try to return it to the store they bought it from, and the person who referred him remembered that he took a much harder line on the practice than the majority of retailers. Similarly, what got Anne Boe on the Phil Donahue show was an oft-repeated wish. For eight years, she got laughs by telling audiences that she wanted to be on the Phil Donahue show. Then she had a good laugh herself when she received a call from Donahue's producer and found out that one of her clients had sent him her video.

Schmoozing with the Media

While the first two steps, meeting people and being memorable, can eventually land you in the path of the media, you can sashay there directly by visiting their watering holes. Larger cities have press clubs that may have events open to the public. In the summertime, writers' conferences abound, and either there or at some other program of a writers' organization you can stay alert for on-the-move freelancers who might view you as their ticket to *American Health, Inc.*, or *Parade* magazines. Parties help, too. About ten years ago I got the opportunity to write a cover story for *Psychology Today* after a friend and I crashed the housewarming party of one of its at-large editors. Peter Desmond, a writer in Cambridge, Massachusetts, who also works as a tax preparer, says he was quoted in the *Boston Globe* because he met a freelance writer at a party who remembered him when she was writing on the changed home-office deduction rules for the *Globe's* real estate section.

Try the time-honored friend-of-a-friend approach if there is a specific writer, host, or magazine you want to approach. A generation before networking came into vogue, social psychologist Stanley Milgram established that you have a fifty-fifty chance of being able to construct a chain of acquaintanceship from yourself to any randomly chosen person in the United States with only two intermediaries. That is, if you're dying to do lunch with NBC anchor Tom Brokaw, syndicated columnist Ellen Goodman, or magazine editor Frances Lear, the odds are one in two that you know someone who knows someone who personally knows him or her. If you find those odds promising, start schmoozing away.

I can't even count the number of times I've interviewed acquaintances, or met people by interviewing them, become friends, and then interviewed them more. In one case, I began doing some editing work for a consultant who decided she wanted more visibility. She asked me if I knew any freelancers who might want to write about her. I gave her the names of three writers who wrote a lot on business topics and she contacted them, but nothing developed. Because I had the chance to learn about her work, however, *I* ended up quoting her in three articles for national magazines. The lesson for her, I suppose, is that familiarity breeds citations.

If the prospect of getting dressed up to work a room strikes dread into you, never fear. Technology now gives you the option of schmoozing with the media while shuffling around at home in your bathrobe. Computer bulletin boards on services like the Internet and CompuServe enable you to cruise through and respond to messages left with special-interest groups, such as mothers working at home, comedians, or craftspeople. Numerous writers locate sources by posting notices on those electronic forums. Paul Edwards estimates that he finds 20 percent of the guests for the *Home Office* show that he and his wife, Sarah, present on the Business Radio Network through the Working at Home Forum on CompuServe. "We also refer people we've met there to reporters who call us," says Edwards. "People have wound up on the covers of national magazines because of contact with us on the bulletin board. Yet when writers leave messages on the forum, the rate of response is nowhere near what it could be. As a general rule, people are missing the boat on opportunities to get media exposure."

Unsocial types can also get on board with the media by taking advantage of free listings of all sorts. For special events, investigate calendar listings in all the papers serving your area, taking note especially of submission deadlines and whether photos are accepted. Send off your vital information for mention in your alumni magazine or organizational, club, or church newsletter. Some trade magazines and others for the general public include resource lists, such as of vocational training programs, computer suppliers, or vacation spas. If you spot such a list that omitted you, contact the magazine and ask if it's a repeated feature and how to submit information for inclusion next time. If you belong to a national or regional professional organization, find out if it maintains a resource database for the media. To locate people to quote for magazine articles, I regularly use the services of the media relations department of the American Psychological Association in Washington, D.C. I call and describe the topic I'm working on, and receive four to six names and phone numbers of association members with expertise in that area who have specifically volunteered to speak to the media.

Less than 2 percent of APA members make themselves available for publicity in this way, however, even though it costs them nothing. If your professional organization does not have such a service, suggest it as a great way to spread awareness of what members do.

If you're more of a joiner, volunteer to be press liaison for any organization you belong to. By becoming a spokesperson or just doing the legwork for a group, you'll get to practice your publicity skills, experience how the media operate, and make contacts you can later take advantage of. With that idea in mind, communication consultant Claire McCarthy serves as the public relations chair for the Greater Lawrence, Massachusetts, Rotary Club. "That means that any time there's an event I'm publicly thanked, and acknowledged in the newspaper. It's elevated my whole credibility in the community," McCarthy says.

Getting to know the leaders of organizations can pay off in publicity, too. For young chocolate maker Kim Merritt, a great organizational go-between with the media came to her unbidden. Someone in the Association of Collegiate Entrepreneurs read about her and contacted her. "Because I was female and one of the youngest entrepreneurs they knew of, whenever ACE sent out press releases, I was one of the people listed," Merritt recalls. A similar connection with someone in the leadership of the National Federation of Independent Businesses led to Merritt being featured in *Money* magazine.

Whenever you do schmooze your way to a good media connection, seize the day. Ruth Jacobs remembers the day an Associated Press reporter showed up at the Wellesley College Center for Research on Women, where Jacobs works, looking for stories about women. "Luckily, I had the presence of mind to give her a copy of my book," Jacobs says. Not only did the reporter gratefully read it, her story went out on the AP newswire and appeared all over the country, with a photo. Likewise, at a meeting of the New York chapter of the National Association of Professional Organizers, Ilise Benun schmoozed with a writer who was working on a piece for *New York* magazine. Benun sent her information about what she did and ended up mentioned in print as someone who helped people promote themselves. "Five years later I'm still getting calls from that article," she says. "It was the type of thing people clipped and saved."

POLISHING
YOUR
PUBLICITY
SKILLS

CHAPTER 14

Getting Reporters on Your Side

Interview shows like *60 Minutes* and *20/20* that seem to show reporters at work actually present a very misleading picture of the job of the journalist. Unless you're a celebrity, public official, corporate spokesperson, or criminal, the reporter will not usually function as your adversary, trying to coax or trick you into revealing information you'd be better off concealing. Instead, the reporter ordinarily tries to get out of you the story or expertise that is yours to share, in a form in which it will make sense to the audience.

Other erroneous expectations may come from horror stories you've heard from others who have been grievously misquoted. But rather than approaching with paranoid apprehension the prospect of being interviewed, you can take steps to improve the odds of being accurately quoted. Also, even indisputable misquotations are not always the disaster you might assume they'd be. Four or five years ago a consultant I know was the subject of a long, front-page feature story in the *Wall Street Journal*. Disgusted at the snide tone and inaccuracies in the story, she showed me a copy of the story with more than a dozen factual errors circled. Yet she also revealed that years later she was still getting calls from potential clients and press inquiries traceable back to that story from as far away as Tokyo. Book publishers have long claimed that any review, even a blisteringly negative one, works better than silence—because it gets the word out. Readers are quite capable of disregarding the writer's attitude and making up their own minds.

As someone who has sat on both sides of the interview encounter, I can clue you in on the agenda, methods, and constraints of reporters as well as preventive measures you can take as an interviewee to ensure that the story ends up serving you. I'll be focusing here on print interviews; Chapter 15 presents additional tips for TV and radio interviews.

Do's and Dont's for Print Interviews

1. *Call the reporter back as soon as possible.* Even more fundamentally, call him or her back, period. For this book, I wrote to twelve individuals who had listings in *Chase's Annual Events*, and of the twelve, only four got back in touch with me within the next three weeks. Since I explained there could be more free publicity in store for these people who had already gone out of their way to get some, I was shocked at the low rate of cooperation. Other journalists confirm this measly record. When Gordon West, a contributing editor for *Boating Industry* magazine, was updating a marine electronics buyer's guide, he contacted eighty-four companies, of which only twenty responded. The other sixty-four missed out on an opportunity for an accurate listing and free editorial space. Putting a journalist first on your list of callbacks or write-backs isn't merely polite. Because every one of them has a deadline to meet, it's essential.

2. *Discuss a mutually agreeable time and place for the interview.* When you receive a call from a reporter, don't assume that you have to begin the interview on the spot. Scheduling the interview at a time convenient for you puts you more in control of the situation. Even if the reporter says he or she is up against a tight deadline, ask if you can call back in ten minutes. That gives you the chance to become mentally and practically prepared.

Although many good interviews take place over the phone, some types of articles and some reporting styles require an in-person meeting. The setting sometimes ends up in the story, so if your office or home won't corroborate the image you hope to project, arrange to meet in a hotel or restaurant instead. If you do suggest meeting over lunch, coffee, or a drink, reach for the check. It sends the message that you understand who's doing whom a favor and that you know reporters don't make princely salaries.

3. *Feel free to set time limits in advance.* If your time is scarce, tell the reporter during the initial call how much you can spare—a half-hour should be plenty for a phone interview, an hour sufficient when you meet in person. Then during the set-aside time don't answer calls or allow other interruptions. Be understanding, though, about the time a photographer needs for a shot worthy of a national magazine. Kim Merritt says that the four or five times magazines like *Money* or *People* have featured her, their photographers spent virtually a whole day at her chocolate factory. "Some people find that bothersome, but I know it helps a lot to have my picture attached to the story. It's making me money as much as if I spent that time with customers," she says.

4. *Ask the reporter's agenda.* Before hanging up from the initial phone conversation, ask something like, "Would you mind telling me the scope and focus of the article you have in mind?" Sometimes in following up on a press release you've sent, the reporter plans a feature article that will spotlight what you wrote about in the release. Other times the reporter merely needs a few additional facts to run a small informative notice. Still other times a topical piece that quotes many people, including you, is in the works. If a journalist has called you on his or her own initiative, it's fair to inquire about the audience, emphasis, and circulation of any publication you're not familiar with, as well as whether he or she is on staff or a freelancer. Freelance writers have a greater chance of their stories getting rejected, but I still recommend cooperation if you can find the time.

Sometimes the reporter's reply will reveal a particular slant that may not be favorable to your business or point of view. If, for example, your release concerned the opening of a new paper mill and the reporter says the article is about the environmental impact of paper mills, warning lights should go off in your brain. Ask more questions, and follow your instincts! You do not have to cooperate with any journalist whom you sense may be biased in advance against you.

5. *Know your own agenda, and prepare.* Before you speak at length with a reporter, get clear on the essential points you want to get across in the interview. Write these points down and have them with you during the interview. A few times people I've interviewed have even handed me their typed list of important points, which I found helpful. Otherwise, just resolve to steer the conversation toward your agenda, gently, if you have to. Study how politicians do this in debates and press conferences. Henry Kissinger once opened a press conference by asking, "Does any reporter have any questions for my answers?"

Preparing at least one example or story for each of your major points beats having to tell the reporter, "Well, let me see . . . Um . . . Gee . . . Gosh . . ." To get ready for her first major interview, *Lions Don't Need to Roar* author Debra Benton thought up as many questions as she could that her interviewer might ask and an effective answer for each, and spread them all out on her desk in anticipation of his call. "I was swimming a lot in those days," she says. "I would swim for an hour and rehearse questions and answers while I was going back and forth in the pool."

6. *Be cooperative during the interview and grateful afterwards.* A writer told me about a man who'd suggested she write a story about him and then sat there like a lunk during the interview, offering little more than monosyllables. I've never encountered that, but I do recall one interviewee who told me how to do my job and a few who complained that I quoted them too briefly. They thereby eliminated themselves from the list of people I would ever contact again. You can stay in your media contacts' good graces by understanding the constraints under which they work.

When a reporter interviews for an article, he or she rarely knows exactly how it will be structured or what the major points and examples will be. That depends on what interviewees say. After gathering information, the writer figures out a way to weave it all together in a way that fits the publication's format, focus, and length. Great quotes from nice people sometimes do not make it into the article. And after the writer finishes with the piece, editors can compel other cuts and changes. Instead of reproaching the reporters because an hour-long chat yielded three printed sentences, thank him or her and express your willingness to be helpful again.

7. *Be specific and colorful during the interview.* General statements, lofty observations, and clichés are useless to a journalist. Speak naturally, but improve your quotability with these media-pleasers:

- *Precise statistics, dates, figures, events, and names.*
  INSTEAD OF: "Most older men worry about losing their hair."
  SAY: "According to the National Council on Balding, one out of every two men over forty has experienced significant hair loss."
  INSTEAD OF: "Pretty soon I was doing all right."
  SAY: "In just half a year I went from ending up in the red every month to making five thousand dollars over expenses every month."
  INSTEAD OF: "I used to be in the hair business."
  SAY: "From 1972 to 1976, I owned the priciest women's beauty salon in North Umberland, called Pinkie's."
- *Fresh ways of saying ordinary ideas.*
  INSTEAD OF: "Well, you know, when the going gets tough, the tough get going."
  SAY: "When I eat my two thousandth peanut butter sandwich of the month is when I always get my best ideas."
  INSTEAD OF: "Everyone needs to look their best at a job interview."
  SAY: "You should dress for a job interview as carefully as you would—no, even more carefully than you would—for your wedding."
- *Interesting examples or stories to illustrate general points.*
  "One of my teachers said I'd either end up on Easy Street or in jail."
  "My at-home wardrobe in those days was mostly the quality-control rejects, regardless of what size they were."
  "When I was seven years old my next-door neighbor, Flossie, was saved from death by emergency surgery. The

day she came home from the hospital was the day I decided to be a doctor."

8. *Spell out and/or explain any unusual terms or names you bring up during the interview.* If your Vice-President of Human Resources is named Sam Smyth—with a "y"—tell the reporter. Monitor yourself for any jargon—words used only by insiders to your field or institution—and explain the meaning of any technical terms that are unavoidable. One artist I know who had created an extraordinary flower garden referred to a man who worked in the garden as her "partner." She was upset when the published article upgraded the man's status to "co-owner," when in fact she paid him to work in her garden and she was the sole owner. She called him her "partner" because they often worked alongside each other pulling up weeds and transplanting bulbs. The reporter probably should have realized it was a leap from "partner" to "co-owner" and checked that with her, but the artist should also have realized that she might easily have been misunderstood, and explained what she meant by "partner." Reporters can't be mind readers!

9. *Don't let anything out of your mouth that you wouldn't want to appear in print.* Some people get so caught up in establishing rapport with me that they say things during an interview like, "Just between you and me—I wouldn't want to see this published . . ." I'm not the kind of person who gets a kick out of turning on the spotlight when someone's pants are down, but how could they know that? Besides, I might stick the taboo information into the article by mistake. A reporter is someone doing a job, not your chum.

10. *Repeat your main points.* "Reporters don't listen very well sometimes," says Alan Weiss. "You can compensate for that by saying the same thing nine different ways." An especially good time to recapitulate key points would be at the end of the interview. Lay out the overall context for your comments as well for the reporter, either at the beginning or the end of the interview. Jeff Slutsky learned this lesson the painful way. In one of his earliest interviews, he told his favorite funny stories to a cub reporter in Cincinnati who took them in a way he didn't intend. "She slammed me, and I have a lot of relatives in Cincinnati who read the article and thought I was some kind of shyster. Luckily

within a year *Inc.* magazine wrote about me and used the very same stories in the right context. I became careful to tell reporters how I use a story, and this works. In the twelve years since then, this didn't happen again."

11. *Don't ask to approve the story before it's published.* Only a very foolish or inexperienced journalist will grant you the right to review the entire article before it's submitted. Since you do have a legitimate concern about accuracy, ask instead that the reporter check back quotes with you. Newspaper reporters, though, may not have enough leeway before deadline to comply. If you have some special concerns that the reporter ought to know about, mention them. For example, a psychologist I interviewed reminded me several times during one interview that he can lose his license if he appears to have diagnosed someone he has not seen as a patient. Therefore it was important that his comments about possible psychological dynamics in the lives of certain public figures be worded in the way he suggested. Not only was I receptive to the reminders, I passed them on to the fact-checking department of the magazine I wrote the article for, alerting them to the importance of not changing certain quotes without checking with the psychologist again.

To help ensure accuracy, I tell reporters at the end of every interview, "If you're not sure about something, please call me back and I'll be glad to clarify it for you." One young reporter was very intimidated interviewing and writing about me, since I'd written a book on writing. She did call me back three times for clarifications, which I pleasantly provided. If I hadn't invited her to call me back, or if I'd been impatient at her first call, the article wouldn't have been as good and as useful to me as it was. I also sent her a note afterwards thanking her for having done a great job—a gesture that can never hurt, even with veteran writers.

12. *Ask to be identified in a way that allows readers to find you.* Don't assume that the reporter will include any of the details you were so careful to enumerate in the press release— your company name, your address, your phone number, or even the precise city or neighborhood in which you're located. If you have a phone listed under your name or your business's name, the minimum would be your name and the city, unless you're "J. Williamson" and the city directory contains five. Sure, some-

one who wants to find you can call all five, but how many would bother? Think this through beforehand, and ask the reporter to include the appropriate identifying information, if possible. According to Joel Goodman, executive director of The Humor Project, when the media make it easier for readers to find you, it's "a win-win-win situation—great for you, helpful for the readers, and a relief for the magazine or newspaper because they don't have to use their staff time responding to inquiries from readers." For instance, when a 1989 *Better Homes and Gardens* article mentioned that readers could receive a free information packet about the positive power of humor in exchange for a self-addressed stamped envelope sent to The Humor Project at 110 Spring Street, Saratoga Springs, NY 12866, 25,000 requests poured in almost immediately and still arrive at the rate of 25 a week. Imagine how long it would take for the magazine to respond to even one-tenth that level of interest!

13. *Don't ask for payment.* Although I've never been asked for money from an interviewee, other writers have been. That's probably the quickest way to get a reporter to hang up on you. Unless you have witnessed the president of the United States in adultery with a minor of the wrong sex and the reporter is from a sleazy tabloid, it wouldn't be done. And it's gauche to ask.

14. *Fax or send collateral information.* A final way you can increase the chances of in-depth, accurate reporting is to fax or send things like your business bio, articles you've published, tip sheets, and other written materials you have on hand. The reporter might use additional examples, stories, and facts from what you send, and refer to it as a check while writing the article. The extra material also makes it more likely that something you didn't mention to the reporter will stick in his or her mind and prompt another call for a related story. Marketing experts say it's easier to keep an old customer than to make a new one; the same goes for your media contacts. Be courteous, cooperative, and interesting, and you'll find yourself quoted more, and more, and more.

If You Do Face Hostile Print Reporters

Janet Jordan, president of Keynote Communications in Cambridge, Massachusetts, says that people can usually get the hang of dealing effectively with hostile reporters in a daylong workshop or just a few coaching sessions. Much of her work consists of preparing executives for situations where the company's credibility might be at stake, such as when activists have chained themselves to the company gate or a fire has broken out at the plant. "The more you know what to expect from reporters, the more confident you'll feel and the more you'll be able to move from a defensive stance to an offensive one," she says. "Remember that whatever the reporter is doing, it's part of his or her job. Your job is to come across as authoritative and credible, and that's a learned skill." Role-play with a friend who pretends to be Mike Wallace or Sam Donaldson, and practice staying alert for these classic reportorial tactics:

- *Goading you to comment on something you really shouldn't discuss.* Never use the phrase "No comment," which has unsavory connotations left over from the days of Watergate, Jordan says. "People will assume you're hiding something. Instead, say, 'I'm not in a position to talk about that,' or explain why you can't talk about it."
- *Trying to put words in your mouth.* Listen carefully when a reporter says something along the lines of, "So what you're saying, in essence, is . . ." If that's not something you'd feel comfortable reading in the paper attached to your name, don't agree. Say "No," then restate the idea in words that do represent your view well.
- *Unfair questions, comparable to "When did you stop beating your wife?"* If you don't agree with the assumptions or information built into a question, say so. Don't get trapped into admitting something that you shouldn't or that isn't true.
- *Asking the same question again and again.* If a reporter persists with the same question, worded a little differently perhaps, you're just as entitled to give the same answer. Don't get

annoyed at being poked in the same place from different angles; stay composed and polite.

• *The silent treatment.* Most people feel uncomfortable with silence. A reporter may pause and look at you expectantly in an attempt to get you blabbing. During a hostile interview, don't fall for it. Just look expectantly back.

• *A friendly chat after the tape recorder or notebook is put away.* As I explained earlier, assume everything is on the record, including anything you say after you think the interview is over. According to Janet Jordan, after interviewing Marlon Brando, Truman Capote told Brando some tales about his sexual escapades while they were walking to the elevator. Brando reciprocated with some stories of his own and then was furious—at himself, it should have been—when that material ended up in Capote's article.

Keep these warnings in perspective, though. If you're a small-time operator making an inoffensive, honest living, the reporter's goal will probably be more in tune with yours—informing, inspiring, or just interesting the public.

CHAPTER 15

Performing on Radio and TV Like a Pro

I made my television debut at the age of seven. The station in New Haven, Connecticut, had a show where a man named Admiral Jack joked around with an audience of kids sitting on bleachers and then showed Popeye cartoons. Occasionally a featured boy or girl would demonstrate a talent by singing or doing magic tricks. One afternoon I stood at the microphone in front of the cameras and read poems I had written.

I recall being intimidated by the waiting room at the station, but not any attack of nerves when I took the spotlight. I must have done fine, because no one in my family remembers it otherwise. Since I was young and so was the medium of TV, expectations were low. By the nineties, however, the typical American adult has logged tens of thousands of hours watching smooth, professional performers on the small screen. In any TV appearance you or I made now, we'd have a lot to measure up to. But there is a simple trick to success on the airwaves, and it begins with a "p."

Prepare, Prepare, Prepare

Find out the format of any show you're scheduled for and watch or listen to it, if possible, to get a sense of the atmosphere. Is it live or taped? Will you be on alone or part of a panel of guests, and if so, who will the others be? Is it a call-in show, or is there interaction with a studio audience? Is the host cozy or confrontational, liberal or conservative? Negotiate ahead of time whether or not they will announce your telephone number, mention a freebie offer, or flash a closeup of your book cover. Ask what you need to do to obtain a tape of the show, and if they say you should bring your own blank tape, find out what kind. Taping is essential to improving your performance. I was astounded to learn from the tape of one of my speeches that a clip-on microphone picked up and amplified the sound of my lips coming apart as I began a thought.

Confirm all the arrangements, date, time, directions, transportation, and parking, in writing—by fax if there's no time for mail. Someone I know was told by her publicist that a show would be taped at 8:00. When she arrived at 8:00 in the morning on the appointed day, however, the studio was all locked up. Puzzled, she went home and learned later that day that the taping would be at 8:00 P. M. Fortunately, she had the evening free. Bring the confirmation sheet with you when you go to the station. I've heard of guests showing up in an office lobby and not having the faintest idea who should be buzzed about their arrival.

You probably already know that white shirts and plaids or other busy patterns won't show up well on TV. Plan what you'll wear ahead of time and make sure your outfit is clean, pressed, comfortable, flattering, and consistent with the image you want to convey. Men, wear over-the-calf socks that stay up, and women, choose a skirt that's long enough that you won't have to worry about the cameras embarrassing you. For radio, leave at home jewelry that makes any noise at all.

At least as important as planning what you'll wear is practicing what you'll say. Don't "wing it"! Decide on the points you want to get across and role-play with a friend who takes the part of the interviewer. Ask the friend to toss you some pre-scripted questions and some out of left field, so you can try leading from an unexpected probe to one of your three main points. Merle Bombardieri says that before beginning her first publicity tour, she rehearsed fitting in the phrases, "In my book, *The Baby Decision* ...," and "When I work with clients, I ...," so that they felt comfortable and sounded natural. If you have to practice without a friend's help, talk to the mirror or play both roles yourself. I can't emphasize enough the difference between actual practice and just thinking about what you're supposed to do. Greg Godek remembers that when he worked in PR, he would tell corporate clients to make just two or three points and keep hammering them home—"but that's easier said than done. When you're actually interviewed, time goes by so fast. It's easy to get carried away with a story, and then the whole thing is over." The more you practice, however, the more likely the rehearsed behavior is to kick in automatically on cue.

For TV, rehearsal should include practicing what you need to do to look good on the video screen. Put a camcorder in the hands of a friend who films you while you speak. Note anything you do that's distracting, which might not be as noticeable in real life. "Hand gestures can look wild on TV," says Laurie Schloff of The Speech Improvement Company in Brookline, Massachusetts. "Your movements should be smooth and controlled. Remember that people will be seeing you large and up close."

As if you were an athlete in training, take special precautions the day of a broadcast appearance. Get enough sleep the night before, and the day of your appearance, don't rev yourself up with too much coffee, try to brace yourself with alcohol or tranquilizers, or consume dairy products, which can make your voice unpleasant, according to Schloff. Eat just enough so that your stomach won't be rumbling and you won't feel sluggish. If you'll be taking part in a taped show, bring along some fruit and a book or crossword puzzle to keep you occupied in case you're kept waiting for hours in the so-called "green room" offstage. This happens sometimes when the station records more than one show in a session.

When You Arrive at the Station

Assuming you've arrived on time, duck into the rest room to repair your windblown hair and make sure you don't have a piece of lunch stuck between your front teeth. Larger TV stations provide guests with a complimentary makeup session—*they* don't look good if your nose is shiny or the pouches under your eyes would make you look raccoonlike on screen. On both TV and radio, many producers or hosts will sit you down for a "pre-interview," in which they go over a few areas they want to ask you about on the air, explain any technical things you need to know, and generally attempt to make you feel comfortable about the interview. Now is the time to hand over your list of sample questions or to ask about anything that concerns you, from "How will I know we're on the air?" to "Who's going on just before me?" They may explain who all the people are who may be scurrying around or, on radio, tell you about the "cough button," which shuts off your microphone if you're desperate to make throat noise. In any case, from the moment you walk into the station, don't touch any piece of technical equipment unless invited to do so.

While you're waiting to go on, the most important thing you can do is to center yourself so that you feel calm (though energized), and ready to be 100 percent present in that studio. "Daydreaming is not conducive to good interviews," says Larry Rochester in his *Book Publicity for Authors and Publishers* (see Chapter 23). "When in front of a microphone or camera, the guest must mentally be there and nowhere else at that time." Rochester describes an extended but simple-to-execute process that enables you to feel and project confidence and well-being and says that it helps him ignore the multitude of just-off-camera distractions at a TV studio. My own centering technique is to place my hand on my lower abdomen, which helps me be composed and steady. While you're waiting is also the ideal time to practice the relaxed, pleasant facial expression you want to be wearing during your first seconds on the air.

Do's and Don't's on the Air

• Once on the air, assume you're always on camera and that your microphone is always on. Without a doubt you will get an urge to scratch a most inconvenient itch; even if someone else is speaking or you think you're still in the middle of a commercial break, restrain yourself. During one of the 1992 presidential debates, some viewers got a bad impression of George Bush when the camera caught him looking at his watch while one of his opponents was speaking. He's the same man who somehow avoided a public relations disaster when he threw up in the lap of the Japanese prime minister, but don't count on being so lucky yourself! Lesser folks have had to scale down their ambitions because of offensive jokes told when assured that the microphone was off.

• Sit carefully and strategically. Lillian Brown, a TV producer and makeup artist who wrote *Your Public Best*, says that while the ideal chair for a talk-show guest would be hard and straightbacked, you will usually encounter "upholstered armchairs, which you can easily cope with by sitting slightly forward on the front edge. Then there is the soft, fat, overpadded sofa, which can be a hazard in that it tends to swallow you up and overpower you. If you sit back in it and cross your legs, you will completely lose control of your breathing and speaking apparatus. You can overcome all that by perching as best you can on the front edge, ignoring the armrests, and finding some way to anchor your body." Whether on radio or TV, avoid any position that might put any part of your body to sleep. It's difficult to be charming and articulate when numbness is spreading along your limbs.

• For TV, be conscious of your body language and facial expressions. Some people frown when they listen or concentrate, and if you don't want to convey disagreement, strive for a neutrally attentive expression instead. Contrarily, a good many people nod their head when they listen even though they disagree, and this is very confusing on television. Save nods for situations where you agree with what's being said.

• Understand the rhythm of the medium. According to Al

Parinello, cohost of the nationally syndicated radio show, *Your Own Success*, the vast majority of guests can do a good interview but not an effective one, because they fail to take into consideration how and why people tune in to radio and TV. To truly exploit your radio or TV appearance, Parinello says, remember first that the audience will change while you speak. On radio, the audience changes from minute to minute and you must repeat yourself rather than assume listeners stay with you. On TV, the audience changes significantly if your appearance crosses the half-hour mark, and you must repeat yourself after the commercial break. Second, you can't simply lift your performance from another medium. "That's the biggest mistake of speakers and seminar leaders—they start to spin a story and then just before they get to the climax, it's time for a commercial break," says Parinello. "Afterwards, the momentum is lost." Third, you need to earn the interest of the audience before you give out your address or phone number or the title of your book. "Not until the audience is saying to themselves, 'This guy is interesting' should you tell them how to get in touch with you," he says.

• Try to match the energy level of your host. "If the host is talking a mile a minute and you answer in a normal speaking voice, you'll sound dopey," says Greg Godek. On the other hand, if the host is a dud, you can pick things up if you put out just a bit more energy, adds Larry Rochester. "Enthusiasm is contagious."

• Give substantive answers, but stay alert to signals from your host that you're talking too long. Szifra Birke calls this her biggest challenge during broadcast interviews. "Some hosts don't want you to say more than two sentences at a time. It's hard for me to be short and compressed, because I like to go on and on. If I'm succinct I can't be engaging, but I'm working on it. You don't look good when the host has to shut you up."

• Remember that you have two audiences: the host you are conversing with, but also, and more importantly, those viewing or listening to the show. Don't get so bent on building rapport with the host that you forget to hook the interest of those tuning in. According to Jeffrey Lant, the electronic media offer the opportunity of a uniquely twentieth-century kind of intimacy that he takes advantage of by addressing his prospects directly when he's on the air, as in, "Now listen up, all you home-based entrepreneurs and people who are thinking of starting a business . . ." Lant explains, "The host is just a prism. You need to talk *through* him or her to the audience. To get a response, talk to the audience about themselves, not about you."

• Use your normal conversational volume. The technicians running the show know how to adjust their controls if necessary.

• Be yourself at your most scintillating. Unless you're a proficient actor, don't try to come across as someone you're not. Audiences don't respond well to phoniness.

Difficult Moments, Special Situations

• *An incompetent or uncongenial interviewer.* Sometimes you find yourself paired with a host or reporter who asks bumbling questions or acts as if he or she woke up on the wrong side of the world. If you want to come off well, you'll have to compensate for their shortcomings without seeming to take over. Laurie Schloff remembers one interviewer who was very cold. She maintained eye contact, a smile, and a warm tone of voice anyway, telling herself, "This person is not going to help me out. I still want to come across well."

• *Remote radio broadcasts.* Many radio shows include the participation of guests by telephone from their home or office rather than from the studio. Whenever you have this kind of publicity opportunity, make the most of it by isolating yourself from interruptions. Put a do-not-disturb sign on your door, keep dogs who might bark or babies who might cry in another room, and most importantly, temporarily disable call-waiting if you have it. (Call your phone company for instructions.) Paul Edwards, cohost of *Home Office* on the Business Radio Network, says that once when he was interviewing a guest by phone, the call-waiting signal came on the line. "Maybe I'd better get that," said the guest. "Please don't," retorted Edwards. "You're live on national radio." Greg Godek installed an extralong cord on his telephone that enables him to stand, walk around, and gesture animatedly whenever he does radio interviews from home. "That really helps me come across," he says.

• *Call-in shows.* The unpredictability of a media interview multiplies when a show includes people who call in and can make brilliant, stupid, relevant, or wildly off-the-point comments. Be as courteous to anonymous callers as you would be to your host. You won't have to worry about responding on the air to any really offensive calls, however. Call-in shows are set up with a seven-second delay that enables the host to cut off anyone making obscene or threatening comments.

• *A panel of guests.* Getting at least your fair share of airtime can become the challenge when you fill just one of several guest slots for the same segment. Knowing the atmosphere of the show beforehand will help you plan appropriate tactics. If the show tends toward brawling free-for-alls, where everyone speaks loudly at the same time and the camera eventually zooms in on the one who is the loudest, politely waiting for your turn won't get you airtime. You'll have to interrupt noisily just like everyone else. On a one-person-at-a-time show, where the host orchestrates contributions, you can graciously cadge extra time by speaking up the instant another panelist has finished, with "May I add something to what Dr. Brothers said?" or "If I can add something quickly . . ." On a radio panel, you can help listeners keep the voices straight if you identify yourself when you break in uninvited. And when Laurie Schloff was promoting our book *Smart Speaking* on a half-hour TV panel segment, I noticed that twice she got extra attention by saying something especially tantalizing just before a commercial break. Both times the host couldn't help saying, "When we come back, Laurie will tell us . . ." Although she says she didn't do it purposely, *you* could.

• *A camera crew at your special event.* In Chapter 12 I recommended that if a news crew comes to you, you should put yourself 100 percent at their disposal. But if a TV crew wants to shoot your special event, you may have to execute a delicate balancing act. Joel Goodman, executive director of The Humor Project, has had video crews from PBS and Turner Broadcasting film his conferences on humor and creativity and says unequivocally that conference participants come first. "I try to head off problems by making sure I talk to the person who would be in charge of shooting on site and going over my concerns. First, I don't want them shining bright lights in the faces of participants. Second, I don't want any cameraperson standing in the way of a seated participant. I also try to get a sense of their goals. The PBS producer was already familiar with my work, and I felt that we were sympatico." The PBS crew produced a stand-alone five-minute spot that was distributed nationally to PBS stations, many of which aired it. As worked out in advance, the Turner Broadcasting crew got more "up close and personal," Goodman says, sometimes filming what felt like four inches from his face. Because they came to a workshop limited to fifty participants, Goodman notified attendees ahead of time. "I thought some people might have concerns, but I told them about my excitement and they were excited, too."

• *Edited segments.* When a reporter for an investigative, news, or magazine-type show comes out with a microphone or camera crew to interview you, he or she will intersperse snippets of what you said with quotes from others. While you have absolutely no control over how much and which parts of your conversation will appear in the report, a simple defensive maneuver reduces the possibility that you'll be quoted with a clip that leaves out your side of the story. Radio and TV editors hate to cut someone off in the middle of a sentence. Thus, couch anything negative you might have to say in a sentence that includes the spin you want listeners or viewers to hear. For example, suppose a confrontational reporter challenges you with, "People who didn't get what they ordered told us that you're a classic ripoff artist." If you protest, "That's not true! We were overwhelmed with demand and everyone eventually got their merchandise," the editor could cut you off after "not true" and before your explanation. If you say instead, "Although it did take some extra time to catch up with orders, we eventually filled them all," the whole sentence will probably make it on the air. Whether or not you're on the hot seat, the more you can deliver concise, colorful "sound bites," the more you'll find snippets of you on the air.

CHAPTER 16

Pitching Over the Phone

In the early eighties, Colorado consultant Debra Benton decided she was ready for serious media coverage and kicked off her campaign with a call to a Chicago-based columnist whose style she admired. "Mr. X, this is Debra Benton of Benton Management Resources in Fort Benton, Colorado," she said. "I know you must get a hundred calls a day from people who say they have a story for you, but I think you really would be interested in what I do." Then she shut up.

"What is it that you do?" the columnist asked.

"People describe me as teaching executives how to have charisma," Benton replied.

The columnist took her number and called her back a week later. They spoke for an hour, and ten days after that she knew his article had appeared because she received a call from a brewery in the Chicago area. The same day she also received calls from both *Time*, which eventually ran its own story, and *Newsweek*, which didn't. Someone else called and hired her sight unseen "for something I would normally have had to work very hard to get," Benton says. Of the dozen and a half calls she received that first day, 80 percent turned into business.

As a direct result of the story about her in *Time*, a printing company brought her to New York City to give a speech. "The company had a very good PR department and sent out releases inviting the media to attend my talk," Benton recalls. Reporters from the *New York Times*, *Barron's*, and *Financial Weekly* attended and wrote her up in their papers. That led to six minutes on *CBS This Morning* and a segment on *Good Morning America*. In addition, both the *Time* and *New York Times* pieces were syndicated internationally, and Benton got calls from South Africa, Germany, and France.

This may sound like a positive version of the nursery rhyme that traces the loss of the war to the want of a nail, but I've given you only a snippet of the results Debra Benton can trace back to getting up the nerve for a thirty-second phone call. If just this much inspires you to want to try you own phone pitch, read on.

Reaching Out to Call the Media

An effective phone pitch to the media starts with the recognition that whenever you call someone associated with radio, TV, newspapers, or magazines, you will be interrupting them. Sometimes they're not just busy, they're hell-bent on a deadline that waits for no one. If you have enough slack to plan the time of your phone call, do. Call the station or publication to learn its deadline and call either way before or just after it. For a monthly, one week a month will probably be most frantic, for a weekly, one day a week will be frenzied, and at a daily show or paper, the pace quickens from crazy to berserk during certain hours.

In preparing to call, make sure you know whom to call as well as when. Usually if you call the main number and ask, "Whom should I call about a _____ story?" (fill in the blank with a category of story, such as business, travel, health, or human interest) they'll give you a name or title and an extension number or direct number. You can also find the names of section editors and producers in many of the directories listed in Chapter 23.

Remember that for radio and TV you call a show's producer, not the host.

Plan a spiel that dispenses with small talk and quickly introduces you and states what the story is that you think will appeal to them. Practice your pitch until you can say it clearly, enthusiastically, and comfortably. "You need to sound better than, more exciting than ninety-five percent of the people who call them," says Stan Billue, a telephone sales trainer in De Bary, Florida. "You'll be more memorable if you rhyme or compare your name, such as 'Evan Gold, like the metal.' People often remember that even years later. Then when you state the purpose of your call, try to provide a benefit for that person's readers or listeners, such as, 'I can share six techniques with your audience that will immediately increase their self-esteem.'"

Go beyond rehearsing your initial pitch by trying also to anticipate objections or noninterested responses. Prepare comebacks that make a second appeal to their interests. According to Steve Schiffman, author of *Cold Calling Techniques That Really Work*, cold calls break down most after the callee responds because the caller doesn't know how to turn around a response in a positive way. "Odds are that the person you're calling won't be interested," Schiffman says. "So if they say, 'Sorry, we're not interested,' ask, 'What kind of stories *are* you interested in?' Then see if you can fit yourself into what they say. Even if only one out of ten people you call responds positively to that, you're still better off than simply hanging up when they say they're not interested."

Stan Billue used exactly that strategy once when he moved to a small town in Florida. He called the nearest paper and said he had an Arabian horse farm and did professional speaking. "Within an hour a photographer showed up at my place," Billue recalls. The paper ran a half-page article with a color photo, and Billue took that to the *Orlando Sentinel*, the major paper for that part of the state. "They said, in effect, that I wasn't important enough for them to do a feature on. So I offered to give them the names of other speakers in the area, and sent a list of all the professional speakers in and around Orlando. Two weeks later they had an article about us in the business section, and almost half of it was about me."

If you take a bit of extra trouble to set up a cold call, you may find that it goes more smoothly. TV producer Lila Ivey says that when she receives a letter or a press kit that includes the line, "I'll be calling you next week," she puts that correspondence in a separate pile to read more carefully. "I want to be prepared when they call, to have an answer ready." When the promised call comes in, she responds with more attention than when an unknown person calls to make contact for the first time.

Nancy Michaels warns not to take it personally if media people seem rude or abrupt—they're just reacting to occupational pressures for efficiency. And don't be discouraged if your first all-out effort goes nowhere. There are tens of thousands of other media people who might respond just as you'd dreamed.

Checklist for Achieving Phone Finesse

Tape-record a practice session and your first few cold calls to the media. If your answering machine doesn't have a record-while-talking feature, you can buy an inexpensive device called a telephone recording control at Radio Shack and elsewhere that easily attaches your phone line to any ordinary tape recorder. (Note: In some states it's a felony to tape a phone conversation without the other party's permission.) Then rate yourself according to the following criteria:

1. *Articulation.* Do your words come across clearly? Since your phone call will be coming out of the blue, you may have to pronounce words more precisely than usual. One person I called while researching this book asked for clarification of the title and told me he thought I'd said "Six Debts," not "Six Steps."

2. *Tone.* Do you sound friendly and natural? Avoid a monotone or sounding cold or computerlike. It may help to imagine the person listening on the other end of the line.

3. *Pace.* You should start right in without fumbling, then keep up an even, brisk pace. Speak a bit faster than you usually do, but don't race.

4. *Relevance.* Do you provide an obvious answer to that all-

important question, Why would our readers/listeners be interested in you now?

5. *Length.* If your opener goes on for longer than twenty seconds, that may be too much. Say just enough to whet the media person's curiosity, and not a syllable more.

6. *Volume.* Can you be heard without strain or recoil? A former colleague of mine used to start her sentences with such a sharp burst of sound that it hurt my ear. If you're too soft, try standing up, which gives you access to more air and breath support.

7. *Intonation.* Do you sound confident? A rising intonation, as in "My name is Marcia Yudkin?" makes you seem tentative and timid.

8. *Poise.* In an actual call, did you have a smooth rejoinder ready when your callee responded?

CHAPTER 17

Ten Pitfalls in Publicity Writing— and How to Avoid Them

Crafting material that will impress the media takes work. Plan to write a press release in two stages: first, a rough draft that captures and develops your idea, and second, a final draft that you've ruthlessly and rigorously polished. Once you're satisfied with content and organization, test your text against this checklist, which will also help you fine-tune any marketing copy, including ads, brochures, flyers, bios, and sales letters. Remember to write press releases and bios in third-person, objective style, in contrast to the "you" that belongs in materials directed to clients and customers. Whatever the occasion, you'll make the most of a reader's limited attention span if you root out the following ten flaws from your promotional materials.

1. *Vague phrases.* Every word and sentence you use should plant a specific meaning in the mind of the reader. But consider these common kinds of statements:

- Hillside Inn is a wonderful place to spend a winter weekend. *(Why is it wonderful? Is it cute and cozy or huge and luxurious? Is it wonderful because it's cheap, or remote, or exotic, or full of media stars on vacation?)*

- Dr. Henry Kissinger has consulted with a variety of individuals and organizations facing unique challenges in many parts of the world. *(If Kissinger put out a press release, do you think these generalities would do him justice?)*
- Addicts Anonymous provides help to people who struggle with their need for various substances. *(Really? If I need enough money to pay next month's rent, or a swatch of fabric to match my grandmother's torn antique shawl, is Addicts Anonymous equipped to help?)*

Compare the following more specific versions of those weak sentences:

- Hillside Inn offers a quiet, affordable refuge from city pressures. *(No product or service can be all things to all people. By being more specific, you increase your attractiveness to customers who will be happy with what you have to offer.)*
- Since leaving the office of U. S. Secretary of State, Dr. Henry Kissinger has advised numerous leaders of foreign governments and multinational corporations on how to adapt to a world rife with terrorism, revolution, and protest. *(Because of the confidentiality of his services, Kissinger might not be able to be more specific than this. But it's an improvement!)*
- Addicts Anonymous provides help to people trying to eliminate their dependence on alcohol, crack or cocaine, marijuana, heroin, amphetamines, tranquilizers, and other harmful or illegal substances. *(That eliminates people needing money or fabric swatches, doesn't it?)*

2. *Negative language.* Notice the difference between these negative assertions and the positive versions that follow each:

Negative: Don't imagine that smart businesspeople shouldn't be aggressive.

Positive: Smart businesspeople must be aggressive.

Negative: Whether or not dieters have already failed with other weight-loss programs, Diet-Eze makes sure that they are not disappointed.

Positive: Diet-Eze guarantees satisfaction with its weight-loss programs.

Negative: Hillside Inn makes it hard for urban dwellers to resist the chance to inexpensively escape the pressures of the city.

Positive: Hillside Inn offers a quiet, affordable refuge from city pressures.

Any negative word, including "not," words starting with "un," "dis," or "mis," "failed," "resist," "escape," "avoid," and so on, forces the reader to perform a mental somersault to arrive at your meaning. As negatives pile up in a sentence, the reader is more likely to become dizzy. Be nice to your reader! You'll communicate more clearly by being direct and positive.

3. *Passive verbs.* As you may recall from high school English class, "Jim hit Bob" uses an active verb, while "Bob was hit," or "Bob was hit by Jim" employ a passive verb. Instead of saying directly who is doing what to whom, passive constructions start off with the whom that is being whatted, and often leave out altogether the who that's doing it. For example:

- Before formulation of a training plan, interviews are generally conducted with problem employees. *(A weak, indirect statement, this doesn't say who conducts the interviews.)*
- Pasta lovers are satisfied by P.L.aghetti's fresh, authentic taste. *(Again, weak and wimpy.)*
- Merchandise can be special-ordered by Boombox City's knowledgeable, helpful clerks. *(This is not only indirect but also unclear. Are the clerks doing the ordering or are they the ones entitled to special orders? Surely you don't want customers confused about that!)*

When you substitute active verbs for passive ones, you get livelier writing. Here are punchier, clearer versions of the above sample sentences:

- Before formulating a training plan, Teletrain's experts interview problem employees and determine specific needs.
- Pasta lovers rave about P.L.aghetti's fresh, authentic taste.
- Boombox City's knowledgeable clerks help customers place special orders for hard-to-find merchandise.

4. *Meaningless superlatives.* Are you fond of words like "best," "newest," and "freshest"? They actually don't carry much credibility unless you explain how your goods or services are the best, newest, or freshest.

- Tri-Tech is world-famous for the newest ideas in high technology. *(Anyone can claim that, can't they? Says who?)*
- Ideal Game Corporation has been one of the major forces in the game world for more than a generation. *(This sounds grand, but how has it been a major force? By suing all of its competitors?)*
- Winsome Widgets, Inc. solves all those quality-control problems perfectly. *(All of them? Even the boss's grandson Benny, who is prone to falling asleep on the job?)*

The following restatements will carry more weight with readers:

- Since 1959, Tri-Tech has received seventeen new patents for technological innovations, more than three times as many as any competitor.
- For more than a generation, Ideal Game Corporation has sent competitors scrambling with games like XXXX, YYYY, and ZZZZ, named "Best Game of the Year" in 1965, 1976, and 1988 by the World Toymakers Association.
- With Winsome Widgets, manufacturers and consumers never need to worry about poor-quality nuts and bolts again.

5. *Jargon.* At a seminar for would-be consultants, I listened carefully as participants introduced themselves and the focus of their consulting. Despite my education and worldliness, I could not understand the self-descriptions given by more than 90 percent of them. They relied on gobbledygook, insiders' buzzwords, and jargon instead of clear, comprehensible language. Yes, you

can use technical terms you're sure that everyone in your target market knows. But "in" language used merely out of habit or to sound superior and "in" leaves many readers out.

- QCA Videos Teach QC Excellence. *(A cute headline, but it's more considerate of readers to spell out "QC" as "quality control.")*
- With strict third-tier sales quotas, TTT's telemarketers get results. *(Maybe people inside your company know what "third-tier sales quotas" are; the rest of the world doesn't.)*
- After ten years as an award-winning high school teacher, Hannah Prood decided to define and implement a career change. *(Just say what it was she did—became a sales trainer.)*

6. *Inconsistencies in tense, person, or voice.* Through carelessness or ignorance, you may be guilty of distracting grammatical inconsistencies. Can you diagnose the problems in these sentences?

- Their special training and experience is geared toward the needs of the customer. *(The phrase "special training and experience" consists of two things and should be followed by "are," not "is.")*
- You need not climb Mount Everest in order for one to deserve a pat on the back. *(You shouldn't mix "one" and "you" in the same sentence, or even the same passage. Choose.)*
- Dr. Kate Hollins-Rollins's odyssey begins in 1952, when she is born to a husband-and-wife team of pediatricians in a suburb of Chicago. In 1980 she received her own medical license. *(Don't mix present tense—"is born to"—with past tense—"received"—in the same passage. Use one or the other consistently.)*

If you couldn't pinpoint and correct those mistakes, I recommend you hire a professional wordsmith to proofread and edit your copy. *Literary Market Place* (see Chapter 23), most writers' organizations, and many university English departments will help you locate editorial assistance.

7. *Wordiness.* Assume that you've used a lot of extra words in whatever you've written, and find them. Search for and destroy all verbal clutter.

Wordy: From twenty-three years of past experience, Martin Goode derived a system of formulating future plans. *(Wouldn't the experience referred to here have to be in the past and the plans in the future?)*

Better: From twenty-three years of experience, Martin Goode derived a system of formulating plans.

Wordy: Needless to say, various different employees follow up on each and every complaint. *(If it's needless to say, don't say it! If it needs saying, say it just once.)*

Better: Several employees follow up on every complaint.

Wordy: Personal coaching is designed to provide individuals with professional encouragement at convenient times. *(Can you find three unnecessary words that weaken and lengthen this thought?)*

Better: Personal coaching provides individuals with professional encouragement at convenient times.

8. *Mistakes in emphasis.* Suppose someone told you, "It'll be easy to identify the important people at the party. They'll be wearing red ties," and at the party *every* man was wearing a *red tie*? You foist a *similar* kind of frustration on your reader when you emphasize *too many words.* Go *lightly* on underlining, italics, extended capitalization, and boldface, and the *rare* word or phrase that *must* stand out *will.* (The reader would understand my meaning perfectly with no italics at all in this paragraph.)

The opposite problem occurs when you bury your most important information in the middle of a paragraph. To make sure your strongest points get the attention they deserve, either lead with them or save them for the end of the paragraph.

Weak: Michael Gepdale, Wysdec's top troubleshooter, brings unique qualifications to his work. He won the decathlon in Olympic competition in 1984 and 1988. Now he puts his energy and persistence at your service.

Stronger: Two-time Olympic decathlon champion Michael Gepdale now puts his energy and persistence to work for you . . .

9. *Clunky, awkward rhythm.* Although people will usually look at your promotional copy rather than read it out loud, prose that would trip up an announcer or sound terrible aloud frequently needs improvement. As a last test of whether you've polished your paragraphs enough, read the whole text out loud. If you have trouble reading any sentence in one breath, it's probably too long. If you hear a series of short, choppy sentences, as you would with the "weak" version in #8, you probably need to combine sentences and vary your sentence patterns. Wherever you trip up while reading out loud, you're likely to have identified a sentence that needs smoothing out. Endings should sound conclusive; if yours don't, tinker with the order of various clauses.

For example, to my ear the preceding paragraph would sound much better if it ended like this: Endings should sound conclusive; tinker with the order of clauses if yours don't.

10. *Absence of credibility-boosting information.* I recently received an invitation to a free evening seminar with a trainer who promised participants measurable improvements in their presentation style. It sounded good, but my question was, Who is this guy? Although he referred to himself as a "renowned international communication and public speaking coach" and he included some testimonials from well-known people, nowhere in his six-page bulletin of seminars or his one-page sales letter did he mention any education, training, or awards in speaking or communication skills. When you leave out credentials, as this man did, readers rightly become suspicious that you haven't any. As you review your publicity materials, look for and remedy omissions that put claims about your qualifications or your products into question.

By the way, did you notice that this whole chapter violates one of the foregoing ten rules? Below is a rewrite that takes account of guideline #2.

TEN KEYS TO PUNCHY, PERSUASIVE PUBLICITY COPY

1. Specific language
2. Positive approach
3. Active verbs
4. Meaningful boasts
5. Phrases understandable by all
6. Consistent grammar
7. Crisp, concise prose
8. Subtle, effective emphasis
9. Lively, forceful rhythm
10. Inclusion of credibility-boosting information

CHAPTER 18

Seventy-Seven Ways for Writers to Get Unstuck When Trying to Write

Writer's block is not terminal—unless you allow yourself to use it as an excuse. Whether you're biting your pen because of an article, a press release, or a brilliant opening line for a pitch letter that eludes you, try one of the following block-breaking strategies instead of simply giving up.

1. Warm up for writing by putting your pen to paper without stopping for at least five minutes, then throwing the paper away.

2. Write a letter to someone about what you would say if only you could get started.

3. Meditate.

4. Stretch and relax.

5. Imagine writing as an obstacle course, then draw it, labeling each obstacle.

6. Interview your obstacle(s), on paper or in your imagination.

7. If you've been concentrating hard, drop the problem; take a walk, do the dishes, go running or swimming, read the newspaper.

8. On paper or in your imagination, interview your future self looking back at how you solved the problem.

9. Notice any particular feelings in your body while you are stuck, describe them precisely, and free-associate about them.

10. Remember times when you succeeded in doing difficult things and give yourself a pep talk: "You can do it. Just try!"

11. Look at the actual results of your past successes; this in itself may pep you up.

12. Concentrate on an ordinary object for five minutes, giving it all your attention; then write about how something you noticed about the object is similar to your problem with writing.

13. Ask yourself, "What are you afraid of?" and write down everything that comes up, no matter how silly or farfetched.

14. Ask yourself what's wrong and write out the explanation with your other—your non-writing—hand.

15. Complete this sentence: "I should be able to . . ." and then ask, "Why?"

16. Try writing in a different, unexpected place: a Laundromat, the kids' room of the library, the train station, the top row of empty bleachers.

17. List all the wrong ways to write your project, and if you get inspired to start in one of the "wrong" ways, go for it.

18. Doodle randomly with colors and see if you can see something in your picture.

19. Find a writing buddy and give each other deadlines.

20. Think of someone you admire; what would that person do now?

21. Read some great piece of writing, put it down, and imitate its style while writing on your topic.

22. Decide on a reward you'll give yourself if you write a page (or even half a page); then get started and really give yourself the reward if you earn it.

23. Sing! (It may wake up a part of your brain you need to use.)

24. Wake up your senses by smelling flowers, looking at art, of listening to favorite music.

25. Make a list: What would you need to know or learn in order to solve this problem quickly?

26. Ask yourself, "Is there any payoff for me in getting stuck right now?"

27. Visualize the problem being gone; then how do you feel?

28. If you had 500 pages in which to tell your story, how would you start? If you had to fit it all on one page, what would your first sentence be?

29. Open your dictionary randomly and without looking, point to a word; use that word in your first sentence and get started, even if it's silly.

30. Talk your piece into a tape recorder.

31. Write a book review, or blurbs, for your book, by real or imaginary people.

32. In your imagination, line up your critics, then put a wall between them and you so you can write without them seeing or hearing you.

33. When you can't think of the right words, make gestures that express what you're feeling, then try to translate them into words.

34. Take a walk and imagine being able to see from the back of your head.

35. Imagine writing or speaking your story to someone who doesn't speak English—or communicate it in gibberish.

36. Ask yourself what color you feel within yourself; if this color were to speak, what would it say?

37. Write sideways, in a circle, or in another pattern.

38. Imagine being the topic or problem: how would you prefer to be written about?

39. Don't sit still to write; pace.

40. List all the solutions to writer's block you've tried in the past; if any ever worked for you, try them again. Think also, though, about whether any of these solutions might be part of the problem.

41. Begin in the middle or at the end if the beginning is too difficult.

42. Wear a patch over one eye; wear earplugs or sound-blocking headphones; block up your nose; wear scratchy or sexy clothes; do a headstand.

43. Breathe alternately through one nostril at a time, a yoga technique that may help you balance both sides of the brain.

44. Take a break and slow down all of your activities during the break (washing dishes, reading the newspaper) to half-speed.

45. Try writing the opposite of what you really want to say.

46. Think of something else besides writing that you are just as stuck on and attack that problem, then see if writing becomes easier.

47. Set a specific time (at least a few days) during which you are not allowed to write the troublesome piece, no matter what (reverse psychology).

48. Turn your difficulty with writing into an elaborate and truly funny sitcom, then think about the truths revealed in the funny parts.

49. When you sit down to write, pretend you are someone else, complete with name, costume, mannerisms, motivation, etc.

50. Use an inappropriate form to record your ideas: a menu, shopping list, computer instructions, legal indictment, dictionary definitions, publicity flyer, personal ad, dialogue.

51. Tell your troubles to a shoe, a pen, or a flower, then sit down to write.

52. When you're procrastinating, make a list: What Am I Waiting For? Then find one item on the list that you can accomplish right away, to break the block.

53. Write it very badly, then see what's salvageable from this attempt.

54. Brag about what a great writer you are, on paper or out loud, then notice any objections, images, or feelings that come up.

55. Ask yourself, "If I did know how to get started, how would I do it?"

56. Write about your attempt to write in the form of a fairy tale.

57. Invent the rhythm for what you want to say, then fill in the words.

58. Find a noun or adjective to describe who, what, or how you are when you can't write: Is that an identity you are trying to hold onto?

59. Consider how much energy you've been expending in not writing.

60. Try writing with colored markers on huge poster paper.

61. With a tape recorder going, have someone interview you

about what you'd like to say, transcribe the tape, and use that as a rough draft.

62. People from planet X understand only pictures and symbols; write something for them.

63. Visit a toy store or a playground, knowing you'll find something there which will help you write.

64. Do something that makes you very bored for twice as long as you think you can stand it, then go write.

65. Think of the writer you could be but are not. What would that writer do? Then do that.

66. Write a letter to The Muse pleading for help.

67. Indulge yourself with your favorite forbidden pleasure, then sit down to write when you're feeling happier.

68. Imagine your writing problem as an opportunity in disguise. If you unmask it, what do you see?

69. Think of the most unreasonable way of writing you can imagine; then modify that in a workable way.

70. Make a "pep tape" of others talking about your real strengths, talents, and triumphs, and play it before you sit down to write.

71. Build a model in aluminum foil, clay, or office supplies of what you are trying to say, then describe in writing what you've built.

72. Find another area of your life where you get things done easily, naturally, and well and transfer strategies you use there to writing.

73. Imagine that you're writing for a brain-damaged reader who can only pick up your meaning and can't notice errors in spelling, punctuation, grammar, or word choice.

74. If you're immobilized by having to correct everything as you go, get two hats, one labeled "writer" and the other labeled "editor"; tell yourself you can't edit when wearing the "writer" hat and vice versa, and switch at increasingly longer intervals.

75. Allow yourself to feel a strong emotion—for instance, anger, grief, love—then immediately begin to write.

76. Examine your stuckness again and again until, like TV's Lt. Columbo, you see something in it.

77. Invent your own way to get unstuck and write me about it.

CHAPTER 19

Getting Sizzling, Forceful Testimonials

One Thursday evening while I was setting up for a one-session workshop at the Boston Center for Adult Education, a woman who had been in one of my other classes burst through the door and exclaimed, "Boy, am I glad to be here!"

I looked at her, surprised.

"I went to the doctor on Tuesday, and he wanted to schedule me for surgery today, but I told him, oh no, it will have to be Friday. I couldn't possibly miss Marcia Yudkin's workshop. I've taken a lot of writing workshops, and you're absolutely the best. You give one-hundred-ten percent. You don't hold anything back."

Heat spread across my face, and my ears began to buzz. If I heard the rest of her accolades, they slipped right on through without sticking in my memory. The idea that someone would postpone surgery on account of my teaching seemed almost beyond belief, and I wasn't sure how to extend sympathy while she was showering me with praise. Other participants began to arrive, and I recovered enough to murmur concern for her health and add in a whisper, "Would you write that down for me—everything you just said?"

She took that right in stride. "You mean as in a recommendation? Sure thing." At the end of the workshop, she handed me a folded piece of paper, and I wished her well.

Had I overstepped some boundary of appropriateness? My nagging worry shifted when I unfolded the paper and read what she had written. Instead of the pointed praise that had made me flush, she had offered three paragraphs of vague raves about my generosity and helpfulness. I smiled and tucked the whole incident away for later reflection.

In retrospect, this episode crystallizes for me some of the challenges standing in the way of testimonials that convey a powerful wallop in your publicity. Even when compelling praise spontaneously comes your way, you have to capture it, and sometimes the process produces embarrassing moments. More often, you have to go out of your way to solicit, collect, save, and purify nuggets of acclaim. But whether you own a car dealership, sell scholarship information, or produce children's parties, whatever trouble you have to go through is usually worth it. Dynamic blurbs inject strength into any press kit, press release, or brochure.

What Makes a Blurb Compelling?

In an effective third-party endorsement, someone offers independent testimony about you, your product, or your service. This testimony persuades insofar as it is attributed, enthusiastic, pithy, and specific. Let's look at each of those four requirements.

• *Attributed.* Floating quotes, attributed to no one, or those credited merely to initials, a title, a company, or a place don't carry much oomph. How will people know that you didn't make them up? At a minimum, testimonials should be accompanied by the person's full name and an identifier, such as a city or organization. The person's occupation or title provide added credibility and help whoever is reading the blurb decide on the relevance of the praise to his or her own goal. For many purposes, blurbs from unknown people and organizations work fine, but your reputation rockets ahead when Dr. Ruth Westheimer endorses your counseling program or the president of the American Truckers Association plugs your antidozing device.

• *Enthusiastic.* The tone of the comments can range anywhere from mildly congratulatory to zealously fervent. Make sure that each word in the testimonial actually carries the weight that the person who praised you intended. For example, the training director who wrote, "We got nothing but good reports about your presentation" undoubtedly meant that as a forceful tribute, but someone reading that might wonder about the weakness of the adjective "good": *only* "good," not "excellent"? When Laurie Schloff and I were collecting blurbs for our book *Smart Speaking*, one of her corporate clients wrote, "It can help you get through the day." Perhaps he meant that the book was so useful you'd want to refer to it for all kinds of different daily situations, but I thought it sounded like the book was for someone who was depressed and dragging through the day. We asked if he would feel comfortable changing that to "It can aid anyone in getting ahead"; he agreed.

• *Pithy.* For publicity purposes, each testimonial should be three sentences or less. But those few sentences need to be as tightly packed as the doll in a jack-in-the-box. The first time I ever tried getting blurbs, I sent a copy of my *Freelance Writing* manuscript to Michael Curtis, an editor at the *Atlantic Monthly*, with a cover letter reminding him of the time we had met. He left a message on my machine saying that he'd written "a couple of sentences" that he hoped would be useful to me. Since I was brand new to the business, I thought, *just* a couple of sentences? But this was what he had written: "Anyone who buys Ms. Yudkin's book can count on a huge return on his or her investment. I don't think I've ever read a dissection of my profession that was as thorough, as fair-minded and as full of genuinely helpful information." In just two sentences Curtis motivated the reader to buy the book with a distillation of its merits. Not only did those two little sentences land on the top of the back cover, they appeared in a box on the publicity flyer and were picked up as the complete description for the book in a catalogue for writers.

• *Specific.* Here is where most of the well-intended commendations you receive fall down. Consider these blurbs, taken from printed materials about various seminars. I've followed each with a question that shows how it could become more powerful.

"The power of this is truly amazing." *(What did the power consist of?)*

"I am proud to say that this seminar has made a real difference." *(In what?)*

"There wasn't a session that I didn't take away something." *(For example?)*

"Really interesting and informative." *(What was interesting about it and what did you learn?)*

"Well done and planned. Results were one-hundred percent!" *(What do you mean by 100% results?)*

Don't despair if getting meaty, pertinent praise is beginning to seem like Mission Impossible. Here are half a dozen tricks that help you pull this business off.

How to Get Blurbs

1. *Unsolicited letters.* Although "unsolicited" means something that you haven't specifically asked for, you can do better than simply sit by the mailbox and pray. When you give a speech, close with, "I'd love to hear from you after you have a chance to apply my ideas." When a customer calls to place an order, say, "Please let me know how the system performs for you." At the end of a column, invite readers to agree or disagree with you. When I recorded my audiotape "Become a More Productive Writer," I ended with, ". . . and let me know what worked for you. You can reach me, Marcia Yudkin, at P.O. Box 1310, Boston, MA 02117. Until then, good-bye." Within two months of the tape's release on the Sounds True label, I received an excited letter from a listener that proved useful to me.

2. *Feedback forms.* You can provide clients with postage-paid postcards to mail back to you with comments or, at a seminar,

ask participants to fill out an evaluation form before they go home. If you're trying to get quotable material, how you word the questions makes an enormous difference. Avoid rating scales like "poor–fair–good–excellent" or "1–10" in favor of evocative questions such as:

- What were the three most valuable things you learned today?
- How would you characterize the service you received at Mighty Motors?
- Would you recommend Dr. Grandview? Why or why not?
- How does Dependable Diaper Deliveries compare with your other options?
- What changes happened in your life as a result of your membership in Live, Don't Diet?

3. *Solicited letters.* I've both called and written regular clients to ask if they would send me a couple of sentences about the specific results they've gotten from working on their writing with me. Almost everyone obliged. Claudyne Wilder, author of *The Presentations Kit,* says that you make the task much easier for people when you give them samples of good blurbs as models. "I like to have a range of quotes, so I might also suggest, for example, 'Would you say something about my teaching style?' " Wilder adds. A bit of flattery encourages cooperation. Wilder called a client she'd done a lot of training for and asked, "Would you be the quote person for my video?" implying that that would be an honor, not an obligation. Similarly, I asked a client if she'd like to be featured as one of my "success stories" on a future flyer. She took it as a compliment. Wilder warns, however, not to promise ahead of time that you'll use someone's endorsement. She did that once, received something that was embarrassingly unusable, and had the author of it call her up and ask why it wasn't on her flyer.

4. *On-the-phone and conversational comments.* If someone offers spontaneous praise, seize the moment and ask, "Can I quote you on that?" Immediately write down their words and get permission to use them. I agree with a framed piece of calligraphy I have that reads, "Writing abides. The spoken word takes wing and cannot be recalled."

5. *Writing them yourself and getting them approved.* Dan Poynter, author of *The Self-Publishing Manual*, says that he has written blurbs himself, called up organization presidents he'd met once, and said, "How does this sound?" He's also used a more elaborate strategy, choosing people with a famous name or recognizable title, sending them a chapter for their expert comments, and then later asking for their seal of approval in a testimonial. "Tell them why their opinion matters," he says. "And emphasize what they might get out of it, like their name on your brochure or the back cover of your book." It seems to me that you have to be an awfully versatile writer to concoct your own blurbs without them all sounding alike.

6. *Facts that substitute for blurbs.* Certain facts carry the clout or cachet of verbal testimonials. Here are some I've seen used:

- Ninety percent of Sam Speaker's speaking engagements represent repeat or referral business.
- Oprah wears them (a make and model of shoes).
- The official birdie of the North American Indoor Badminton Association.
- One of only seven people in the world to receive the designation "Master Page-Turner."

Without any specific words of praise, these imply endorsements and can come in handy in press releases and press kits.

The Ethics of Editing and Using Blurbs

"Nice guys finish last."
"War is hell."
"What's good for General Motors is good for the country."
Are you shocked to learn that none of these hallowed sayings was uttered exactly as we now quote them? In tracking down famous quotations for his book *"Nice Guys Finish Seventh": False Phrases, Spurious Sayings, and Familiar Misquotations*, Ralph Keyes discovered that Leo Durocher, manager of the Brooklyn Dodgers, actually said, in talking about the New York

Giants, "The nice guys are all over there. In seventh place." General Sherman in fact used a lot more than three short words: "There is many a boy here today who looks on war as all glory, but, boys, it is all hell." And the wimpier but authentic words of Secretary of Defense Charles E. Wilson were, "For years I thought that what was good for our country was good for General Motors and vice versa." Reporters and speechgivers afterwards molded interesting thoughts into electrifying ones. And the lesson that I draw from this is: So can you.

As long as your testimonial writers are alive, you should ask for their agreement with your snappier version of their words and indeed with quoting them at all if the comments were unsolicited. Someone I know sent a copy of her book to a public figure, received a warm personal letter of thanks, and then excerpted the letter in all of her publicity. That doesn't sit right with me. Since the blurb derived from private correspondence rather than from public comments or from a context in which it was clear that the comments might become public, I think the well-known person deserved the right to say "yes" or "no" to being quoted. I understand that in some states it's even against the law to use someone's comments for commercial gain without permission. The same goes for condensing and polishing remarks that the maker did know were for a quote. You don't want people who'd been saying nice things about you hollering, "Out of context!"

In addition to the four criteria I listed earlier in this chapter, when you edit blurbs, pick out the strongest ideas and get rid of all unnecessary words and any repetitions. If the wording sounds stiff or unnatural, call up the writer and ask him how he'd express that idea over a beer to a close friend or colleague. And insert enough context so that outsiders know what the testimonial is praising.

For example, I received an unsolicited letter from a woman in my magazine-writing workshop. Here it is, unedited:

Dear Marcia,

You asked me if I can now respond, "I'm a writer." Well, I guess the answer is, yes.

While I already "got my money back," the more important thing is I do feel purposeful and productive in my identity of creating my own work (rather than being employed by another). Hopefully, that will pay off for the rest of my life.

I enjoyed your classes and hope to see you again sometime.

Kathi P. Geisler

The first step toward turning this thank-you letter into a testimonial is deciding which parts carry the most weight. To me, someone predicting that a ten-session workshop will pay off for the rest of her life is pretty strong. So I would make that the central idea of the blurb. Next, I would ask myself if Kathi left out anything that might help the reader appreciate her comments more. She didn't mention that she got several articles published that she'd brought to the workshop, so with her permission I would add that. Putting that together with the identity theme in two or three punchy sentences yields the following:

While attending your freelance writing workshop, I got my first paid articles published in newspapers. Not only can I now call myself a writer, I feel confident about being able to create my own work, rather than being employed by another. I think this will pay off for the rest of my life.

—Kathi P. Geisler

Note that I could have just as well put this paragraph in third person—"As a result of Marcia's freelance writing workshop . . ." Finally, I needed to call Kathi, explain my editing, and ask her approval for the blurb. (I did, and she agreed.)

Some people get hung up on getting a strong, concise, pertinent letter signed by the endorser on company letterhead. While this looks great framed in a waiting room, it's unnecessary and even counterproductive for the media. Reporters would rather have a dozen testimonials bunched together on one or two pieces of paper than a dozen pages they have to spend time and energy flipping through. An attractive quote sheet (see Chapter 5 for a sample) makes a better impression when it's faxed, too. And once you've passed the gauntlet of your first few print interviews, you'll have less room in your press kit for individual endorsement letters.

CHAPTER 20

How to Concoct
Creative Angles, Images,
and Exploits

So I've convinced you that you need an original idea to earn media coverage for your ordinary old pick-your-own-apples apple orchard. But you're stumped. Your thoughts feel like sludge, the only possibilities you've come up with bore you, and disgust is growing by the minute.

Then it's time to go ahead and give up. Stop trying so hard! Stop trying, period. Creativity goes into hiding when willpower is out flexing its muscles. Let go of the problem completely and do something else. If that feels too undirected, just before you quit, send a message to your unconscious mind that sometime in the next few days, you'd like to have a brainstorm. Then answer your phone messages, eat lunch, go out to the floor and serve customers, or do whatever else needs to be done. Later on, when you're biting into a french fry or punching numbers into the cash register, a clever headline will probably whisper in your ear or flash onto your mental video monitor. If that age-old proven method doesn't yield a "Eureka" when you need it, however, don't worry. Use the creativity kindlers in the rest of this chapter to discover the spark that will light a fire under the media for you.

The Metaphor Game

One of the easiest and most effective ways to make a same-old-anything sound fresh is to describe it using a metaphor—a figure of speech that compares something ordinary to something more surprising, funny, or exotic. The books *Guerrilla Dating Tactics*, *Guerrilla Marketing*, and *Guerrilla P.R.*, for example, each compare something that doesn't literally involve gunmen hiding in the hills with guerrilla warfare. I used a cooking metaphor in the following lead of a press release about an otherwise not-that-newsworthy conference:

"Business for Boston, Massachusetts," a conference at Northeastern University on June 19 and 20, offers a compelling recipe for aiding the troubled regional economy: Take more than forty of the largest New England purchasers, from Raytheon and Massport to Digital and ITT Sheraton. Add representatives of several hundred local companies capable of fulfilling their needs. Mix in an educational setting designed to maximize exchange of information about needs and procedures. Estimated yield: $40 million of new orders for participating small, minority and women-owned businesses based in the area.

Far from yawning, the *Boston Herald* sent both a reporter and a photographer and ran a big spread on the second day of the conference.

Taking off on a traditional parlor game, I've devised the following questions, which will help you come up with numerous metaphor candidates. Some people get their best results when they close their eyes after each question. From all the images and words that come up, choose and develop the metaphor that excites you most and suits your purposes. Feel free, of course, to scrap my list and make up your own—or just let yourself fantasize without any trigger questions.

1. If your product, service, or message were a vegetable, which one would it be?

2. If it were a job, which one would it be?
3. If it were a kind of weather, which kind would it be?
4. How about a tool?
5. A temperature?
6. An animal?
7. A smell?
8. A crime?
9. A toy?
10. Something to wear?
11. A country?
12. A spare-time activity?
13. A sound?
14. An exact time of day?
15. A department in the supermarket?

Turnaround Is Fair Play

List at least twenty clichés and see how many you can twist into an angle. Here are half a dozen tired phrases and sayings to get you started.

- "George Washington slept here."
- "You can never go home again."
- "A stitch in time saves nine."
- "Boys don't make passes at girls who wear glasses."
- "That's a bit of a sticky wicket."
- "It's not over until the fat lady sings." (*Aha—we could stage some sort of a closing ceremony with a plump soprano providing entertainment.*)

Borrow for the Morrow

Letting successful publicity inspire you is smart. Echo what someone else has done, but in a different key or on a different instrument.

1. Analyze the appeal of bestselling products or movies, especially those you and your target market like and respect. Any

ideas about what you could do or say that, without copying, would borrow that appeal?

2. Read trade magazines for a business area that seems leagues away from yours. If you design fabric, who's making news in accounting and why—and can you try something similar?

3. Pick up the newspaper and articulate why each story on the front page landed there. Then invent similar headlines and stories involving you. Examples:

MICROSOFT AND 2 CABLE GIANTS CLOSE TO AN ALLIANCE: *Oh, maybe I could form an alliance with someone everyone thinks is in a different business.*

HIDDEN ECONOMY: IMMIGRANTS UNDERGROUND: *Hmm, what's the underside of the law? Fee-padding? Maybe I could explain the innovative steps we take to avoid overcharging clients.*

CITY LEADERS HOLD LINE ON TAXES IN THE CITY BUDGET: *Let's see, suppose I held a line in price increases . . .*

Imagine That!

Playing "what if" has paid off for innumerable inventors and authors. How about for you?

1. Suppose you could afford a famous spokesperson, alive or dead. Whom would you choose?

2. Imagine a scenario in which your product saved the world, or, a little less modestly, in which it earned a presidential proclamation. How might it do that?

3. Pretend you're serving ten additional audiences you don't particularly pay attention to now. What would they be, and which might have news value?

4. Suppose the only legal medium for publicity was a sandwich board on which you could paint one picture or up to five big words. What would you put there?

5. If you were doing what you do now in prehistoric times,

what would that be like? How about in Bora Bora? Or on the fourth moon of Jupiter?

6. Complete this story: *"Once upon a time there was an enterprising young lass (or lad) named _____ who had _____ ed and wanted the whole kingdom to know about it. So she (he) . . ."*

Funny Stuff

Laughter loosens the lid on creativity. Joel Goodman of The Humor Project calls this "the HAHA-AHA! connection."

1. What do you say to yourself or others about what you do that gets rueful, jovial, or sidesplitting laughs?
2. If someone were to poke good-natured fun at you in a spoof, how could they do it?
3. Imagine a humorous commercial featuring your organization. Might a toned-down version incorporated into a press release interest the public?
4. Suppose you had to act out what you do and what's so special about it according to the rules of Charades. How would you do it?
5. Ask a kid who knows you what he or she imagines that you do all day. Or ask a whole carpoolful of kids how they would spend the day if they were running your organization.

Ear to the Ground

Sometimes the very idea we need passes by in disguise. If we pay careful attention, we're more likely to recognize it.

1. What are the stories you or patrons tell over and over again about yourself? What do these show? Is there a tantalizing thread running through them?
2. Take out last year's appointment calendar or annual report. Did you do something last year that deserved to be publicized?

3. What are the complaints you hear about competitors that no one hears about you?

4. Which emotions motivate your devotees—fear? pride? impatience? hope? Is there a story there?

5. Eavesdrop on your audience. Is there something you know about them that they don't seem to know?

Impromptu Performances

In my creativity seminars, participants perform an improvisational exercise in pairs. While standing up, person A pretends to hand person B something, which person B pretends to take. Person A asks person B, now holding the object, a series of unscripted questions about the object; person B makes up the answers, whatever feels right at the moment. For example:

A: Hey, I read something about you today in this magazine here. (Hands it to B.)

B: (Takes the magazine.) Oh yeah?

A: Yeah, look on page 37.

B: (Turns pages.)

A: What does it say?

B: (Pretending to read.) It says I just got elected chairman of the Recycling Society.

A: Does it have a picture?

B: Yeah, it shows me together with a sculpture made out of crushed aluminum cans.

A: How did you get into the magazine?

And so on. So long as A keeps asking questions and B answers spontaneously, this becomes fun, easy, and revealing. After a few minutes A and B switch roles. A variation would be for A to say, "Hey, I saw you on TV today," and hand B the VCR remote for the tape.

If you can't find a friend to try that with, another of my seminar exercises works well for one person. Sit down with a piece of drawing paper and crayons or colored markers. Using two different colors, draw any two shapes or lines. Then turn the paper upside down. You now have before you the beginnings of a picture of how you finagled free publicity. Pick up your crayons or markers and, without thinking about it, complete the picture. Then give it a caption.

Both this and the improvisational exercise coax your unconscious mind to come out with its perspectives on how publicity might emerge naturally and comfortably for you. Whichever of these creativity-kindlers you use, take note of any responses that make you laugh or send a chill down your spine. Those are the ones that, refined, hold the potential to strike home with the public.

Making Time to Publicize

When Dwight D. Eisenhower became president, he decided he would fulfill his duties with the utmost efficiency. Top priority every day would be those matters that were both urgent and important. Eisenhower had to jettison his resolution, however, when he discovered that what was urgent rarely was important, and what was important rarely showed up as an urgent problem.

You'll probably find that Eisenhower's lesson applies to your experience in finding time to do publicity. Although publicity offers important benefits, it rarely presents itself as urgent. If you constantly concentrate on immediately pressing tasks, like answering client calls, preparing UPS shipments, and arranging payroll, you may not get around to taking the steps that lead to valuable media publicity. No one system will solve this problem for everyone, so as you read the suggestions in this chapter, notice those that appeal to you and begin taking advantage of them right away.

Three Models for Getting Around to Publicity

Making time to publicize might mean making it your number-one priority for a brief time period, or focusing on it regularly along with everything else you do. Here are the advantages and disadvantages of three different approaches.

1. *Steady drops of water.* Just as salespeople know that they need to make a certain number of cold calls per day to find new customers, you may decide to put publicity-seeking on your agenda every day that you work. John Kremer, author of *1001 Ways to Market Your Books*, says that he aims at doing five promotional things a day. "This might mean calling someone, writing a letter, mailing a review copy, asking someone for a blurb. Because I've made it a habit to be always thinking about publicity and always looking for opportunities, I get more ideas that aren't obvious." Spreading publicity efforts out within your regular routine may make it easier to spare the time. However, this method may preclude the big push that could accompany a grand opening, product release, or special event.

2. *Waves.* Instead of working on publicity every day or every week, you can set aside time a few times a year for intensive publicity efforts. This approach especially makes sense if your business or organization has seasonal activities, special events, or periodic new services or products. But it also works well if you're the planner type and set annual goals for results you'd like to see. Schedule in, for example, Wave #1 at the end of February, Wave #2 in May, Wave #3 in August, and so on. If your business has a slow time of year—for example, most of December for trainers or the dead of winter for some retailers—use that time to write press releases, compile your media list, or do your newsworthy customer survey. However, by putting publicity out of mind when it's out of your schedule, you might miss some opportunities, such as articles that provide a good pretext for a letter to an editor.

3. *Tsunamis.* Once every couple of years you might find the energy and stimulus to launch what Jeffrey Lant calls a tsunami—a tidal wave of publicity. Here you're so confident of

your newsworthiness that you minimize your other activities and go all out. You make phone pitches, follow up calls, and schedule interviews until you're teetering on exhaustion. The effort Norman George put out to reach ten million people about his Edgar Allan Poe anniversary celebration was, for him, a once-in-a-very-long-while event. If you're releasing a book that you're determined to make a bestseller or mounting a demonstration that you hope will change minds and laws all over the country, a tsunami may be in order. Usually a tsunami creates ripple opportunities that you'll want to take advantage of, though, instead of just drying out afterwards.

I use a combination of approaches #1 and #2. I send out press releases every few months, on average, and in between collect ideas, inspirations, and information about the media to use in my next wave. Hence, besides timing, my approach requires effective systems for saving material between waves.

Getting and Staying Organized

For publicity, my most important system is my way of catching and saving ideas. All of the possibilities that pop into my mind while reading or puttering around I write down in one place, a bound notebook. When I execute one of those ideas, I check it off. Once in a while I'll reread the list and see what jumps out at me as something I could get moving on now. While this may seem like a boringly simple system, I find it invaluable to have all the ideas gathered in one place rather than scattered to the winds on scraps of paper. If you're an inveterate scraps-of-paper type, I recommend at least designating a file or shoebox for storing them together.

Another thing to collect is other people's ideas. Clip articles about people in any field at all whose media coverage catches your eye or makes you marvel out loud. People in the advertising business call this a "swipe file." Of course, you won't steal and you won't copy exactly; you'll borrow and adapt—perfectly kosher and legal.

Third, I recommend you have a place to collect and save information about periodicals, shows, and reporters that seem to be interested in your topic area. I've finally set up a computer file for this, having realized that keeping this information in seven different places (one of which is nowhere) only makes lots more work for me.

Fourth and finally, keep a file for copies of all the publicity materials you draft or send. In 1980, when the calendar was running out on my assistant professor job at Smith College, I dashed off a letter to the *New York Times* Education Supplement offering to write an article. Not only did the Education Editor call me the day he received the letter, he accepted and published the article I wrote, which subsequently opened up other opportunities for me. Since this happened in the days before computers and I didn't bother with a trip to the copy shop before I dropped the letter in the mailbox, I don't have the text of what unexpectedly launched my second career (although I do recall my opening line). If your press release or public service announcement leads to fame and fortune, wouldn't you want to have saved it? Remember: you never know.

Problems and Solutions

Do you wait and wait and wait and wait because you want your release or phone pitch to be sensational? Then you need a way around perfectionism. If you've written something, set it aside overnight and proofread it carefully. Then, if you can't pinpoint any fixable flaws, tell yourself there aren't any and send it out. Or put someone dependable in charge of quality control and have him or her declare the readiness of your stuff to go out. The same goes for an oral pitch: practice, and then ask for a thumbs-up/thumbs-down assessment from someone you trust. If it's a "go," stop practicing and do it.

Suppose you'd like to try a publicity wave but simply can't carve out time amidst your other responsibilities. Actually, much of the work involved in putting out, say, a press release can be done while you're doing something else. Divide the steps into tasks that are creative and those that are routine. Apply yourself to the creative steps, like thinking up an angle, while you're doing something that requires only partial attention, such as driving to work, scrubbing the deli counter, or mowing the lawn. As I explained in Chapter 20, inspiration probably won't come immediately, but even a half-brained stint of attention to the problem hastens a solution. The routine steps, such as folding and stamping releases, you can do during the nightly news or while a friend or family member has stopped in for a chat.

Does the whole process feel overwhelming? Then start out with the smallest, least time-consuming step. Or contact the placement office of a local college to find an intern with an interest in business, journalism, or communications. An intern works on a project part-time for you in exchange for experience to put on his or her résumé, college credit, or both. Given a copy of this book, any reasonably intelligent and motivated college student should be able to execute a publicity campaign for you.

Are you an inveterate procrastinator? Try the buddy system: With a friend or colleague, set deadlines and keep each other on track with either encouraging or guilt-tripping phone calls—whichever works. Or promise yourself rewards just for getting mobilized (the publicity you receive after getting going will be a bonus). And then there's one of my favorite approaches. A fencing coach whose team wasn't doing their daily jogging got team members to promise simply to put on their running clothes once a day. Everyone found it easy to make and keep that promise. Then once they were dressed to run, it felt simple and natural for them to head on out and do three miles. You could adapt their success by resolving merely to take your list of publicity ideas out of the drawer once a day and look at it.

Ilise Benun, president of The Art of Self-Promotion in Hoboken, New Jersey, told me about a startling discovery she made when she began helping clients as a professional organizer. "I would start going through piles of paper with someone, and inevitably at the bottom of the pile there would be some self-promotional thing that they could never bring themselves to do. For example, someone wrote to them asking for information and they just couldn't answer." Why? Her answer is worth thinking about if you say you want to launch publicity for yourself, then take a step or two, and never get around to following through. "Organizational disaster, I found, is usually a cover for fear of putting your work out into the world."

Reread Chapter 3 if Benun's words hit home.

KEEPING THE PUBLICITY MOMENTUM GOING

CHAPTER 22

Capitalizing and Building on Your Free Publicity

Andy Warhol, who received plenty of publicity during his life for both his art and his personality, once said, "In the future, everyone will be world famous for fifteen minutes." Once you receive your first fifteen minutes, you'll probably want more, and like Warhol himself, you certainly do not have to remain content with that small portion. For a sustained, expanding media presence, commit yourself to a long-term effort and follow a few simple guidelines.

How to Stretch Fifteen Minutes of Fame to a Lifetime

1. *Create and maintain a relationship with the media.* Write thank-you notes to people who have written about you or put you on the air. Talk-show host Al Parinello says that of the 2,500 guests he's interviewed, only 10—less than 1 percent—wrote to thank him afterwards. Send media contacts more information about what you're up to from time to time, whether in a per-

sonal note with your next press release, a brief letter along with your new product brochure, or a postcard from Iceland, where you're participating in a trade show. Among the people I interviewed for this book, I could tell the real pros at publicity because they asked for my address and phone number for their records, wanted to know more about the kind of writing I did, and sent follow-up materials promptly whether or not I had asked for them. Others just did the interview and asked when the book would be out. A few said they didn't have time to be interviewed. I'll have more to say about the last group in a bit.

As you should with any important career contact, try to give and not just get. After Ethel Cook, a Bedford, Massachusetts, consultant on office-management issues, got a write-up about her time-management ideas in *Entrepreneurial Woman*, she sent the editor who had made contact with her clippings about other interesting businesswomen from time to time. "It keeps my name in front of her," Cook explains, "and it gives me a chance to spread the wealth. I do think it will come back to me, but if not, that's okay, too." Similarly, Claudyne Wilder thinks that one of the reasons her book *The Presentations Kit* was featured in a nationally syndicated review column was her attitude when the columnist called her up. "I'm convinced most of us talk too much. I try to be gracious and listen and not just talk. I took the approach, 'Who are you, what do you need, and how can I help you?' " she says. "I suggested other books he might want to review."

2. *Don't turn down publicity opportunities.* Saying "I'm too busy" when someone from the media calls you makes about as much sense as saying "No, thanks" when someone says, "I'd like to give you a few thousand dollars of free advertising." Yet one nationally prominent consultant did essentially that when I requested a twenty-minute phone interview for this book. First she set up an appointment for three weeks later; the day before we were to talk, her assistant called to cancel (not reschedule), relaying this answer to my question of what the firm had done to get publicity: "I'll guess we've just been lucky." They'd be much, much luckier if they gave the press higher priority!

Compare the attitude of Steve Schiffman, who returns media calls even during the days he's on the road presenting seminars. "I tell people we have to take a break because I have to give some quotes to *Success* magazine, and they love it. I got the contract for my second book, *The Consultant's Handbook*, because my editor called and said someone else was supposed to do it but she was too busy. Why on earth would you turn down something like that? I'm always available when someone else pulls out of an interview, whether it's nine o'clock at night or whatever." Similarly, Jeffrey Lant told me that years ago he put the word out that he'd be available at any time when someone else cancelled, and radio and TV producers did call to ask him to fill in. "Even if I was asleep or sick, I did it."

I've thought a lot about this "no time for interviews" stance, and concluded that it must come from fear, ignorance about the benefits of publicity, or an unthinking rigidity about fitting interviews around other obligations. Keep in mind that few magazine or newspaper reporters or book writers keep nine-to-five hours. Are you sure you can't find twenty minutes in the evening instead of watching the news? One woman crunched away on her lunch while I interviewed her—fine with me. A man once instructed me to call him on Christmas Day at his in-laws' house—I worried what his wife's parents would think, but I did it. I've not yet interviewed someone speaking from their car phone, but that would be another possibility. If you really do want the benefits of publicity outlined in Chapter 1, then make time when opportunities arise.

Even if the opportunity seems a small one, seize it. Both Janet Jordan of Keystone Communications and Ethel Cook were featured in *Entrepreneurial Woman* because of articles by or about them in the *New England Women Business Owners* newsletter, which circulates to just a few hundred people—including magazine editors on the other coast. Similarly, an obscure talk show can be rebroadcast elsewhere and, as social worker/ author Merle Bombardieri says, "You never know when a producer or host will get a job with a bigger station and remember you. It happened to me."

3. *Keep a file of clippings.* The surest, and most expensive, way to get copies of what people write about you is to subscribe to a clipping service, which usually charges a monthly fee plus a certain amount per clipping forwarded to you. You can find a national list of clipping services in your library's copy of *Literary Market Place*. Until you're being quoted several times a

week, you might as well try to track them down yourself. You can try asking the journalist who interviewed you to send you a copy of the completed piece, but they often can't or won't. You can also ask when the piece is scheduled to appear and how you can order a copy of the publication. Usually newspaper reporters will give you the phone number of the "back copies" department, which charges you a dollar or so for a copy of the paper from a specific date. If you write down the name and number of the reporter, you can call him or her after the date the article was to have appeared to confirm the date so you can order the copy on your own.

Once you have a copy of the published article, paste it up attractively, cutting it away from any surrounding advertisement and arranging it concisely on as few pages as possible. A good print shop will know how to copy newsprint without including type from the opposite side of the page or lines marking the edges of the article. Keep the original in a safe place! I used one clipping as a tip sheet and made copies of copies of copies so many times that it's become unreadable. I now have to retypeset it if I want to use it again. Most people paste up their press clippings with the publication's masthead—the distinctively styled title from the top of the front page—and eliminate the publication date after a year or so has gone by. You can obliterate other inconvenient contents, too. From the feature article about him in the *Wall Street Journal*, Jeff Slutsky "whited out" the prices he was then charging and the name of his former business partner. With widely available desktop publishing equipment, you can even match the typeface of the publication and reset the article yourself to facilitate omissions of sections that are irrelevant to you or to correct distressing typos. Although many people duplicate their press clippings on heavy, glossy paper, regular copier paper does the job, too.

If you have a storefront or a waiting room, consider mounting and framing your clippings for the edification of customers or clients. I know that if I'm scouting restaurants in unfamiliar territory and see a review posted in the window next to the menu, it makes a difference. Otherwise, include copies of your clippings in your press kit and send new ones with an attached personal note to potential clients and others.

4. *Keep a list of radio and TV shows you've participated in.* As this list grows, it becomes another valuable addition to your press kit. Recontact the producers periodically with new ideas to see if they'd like you to return to the show.

5. *Consider creating tip sheets or other enticements for readers and listeners to get in touch with you.* By telling a reporter or producer about something you'd like to offer for free, you may accomplish two things: you'll hear directly from people who might be excellent prospects for your products or services and when you hear from them, you'll know roughly when and where material about you appeared. With newspapers particularly, an item might be written up originally for one paper and then through syndication show up later in many others. When syndicated business columnist Michael Pellecchia interviewed me about my work on creativity, he mentioned at the end of his article that anyone willing to fill out a two-page questionnaire about their creative process could send a self-addressed stamped envelope to me at my address, which he provided. I received more than 200 responses after his piece appeared in Fort Worth, Texas; Des Moines, Iowa; Newport News, Virginia; and Minneapolis, Minnesota. TV and radio shows will often consent to mention your address and/or phone number, and in the case of TV, flash it on the screen—if you ask. According to Jeffrey Lant, although many radio and TV people shrink from giving out addresses on the air, if you're offering something free to listeners, even PBS will often agree to give out the details.

6. *Try to maintain a stable address.* If by the time a magazine article about your successes in Phoenix comes out, you've moved to Atlanta, your publicity will have less impact. One solution I discovered when I moved from Boston proper to a town ten miles away is maintaining the old phone number and telephone listing and having calls automatically routed to the new phone, which you can do for as long as you like, for a reasonable fee. Because print publicity in particular can stick around in files and libraries for years, I think this problem is worth solving. I attribute $7,000 of business to one phone call that reached me because a book of mine said I lived in Boston and someone was able to find me through directory assistance there.

7. *Recycle your publicity materials.* I don't mean tossing your clippings into recycling bins, but constantly looking at ev-

erything you've done to see how you can get double or triple use out of them. If you've come up with a fresh, fascinating hook for a press release, can you turn it into a tip sheet or a seminar? If a topic for a lecture pulled an overflow crowd that couldn't stop asking questions, why not propose it for a radio call-in show? Letters to the editor can become press releases or op-ed pieces, while an appearance on a talk show becomes a pretext for a notice in your alumni magazine and local newspaper. Or how about digging articles you published years ago out of your files and pondering how you might update them for a book proposal?

8. *Assess your successes.* Try to analyze what went right and why and use that knowledge for your next media campaign. If you build up a comfortable rapport with a reporter or producer, you can even ask what about your release made him or her contact you. Michael Pellecchia, the business columnist I referred to above, mentioned that he'd never heard of a creativity consultant who worked not with companies but with individuals. That hadn't even occurred to me as something noteworthy about what I was doing. If one press release gets a tremendous response and another nothing, mull over possible reasons and form hypotheses: a headline was weak, the timing was off, the angle wasn't distinctive enough.

9. *Let me know what worked for you.* Please send me copies of any press releases that worked, along with a note about your results, to Marcia Yudkin, P.O. Box 1310, Boston, MA 02117. In future editions of this book or other writings I may want to share your success with others—which would mean more free publicity for you. If you follow the guidelines in this book and don't get results, please let me know about that, too. You may be making some easily remedied mistakes, and I'd be glad to serve as your consultant to pinpoint the problem and improve your approach.

And don't get too busy to celebrate any sort of publicity coup. The glow of passing the word to the public about you or something you believe in can be warm and sweet. Enjoy it.

CHAPTER 23

Resources for Your Publicity Campaigns

I'd be glad to do my best to put you in touch with any person mentioned in this book. To receive the address of anyone I interviewed, just send me a self-addressed stamped envelope and the name of the person or company you'd like to contact.

Important Library Reference Works

Virtually every library carries at least some of the following resources. Besides your hometown's public library, investigate the holdings of nearby college and university libraries, whose reference facilities are often open to anyone who walks in. You should also know that if you have one quick reference question, such as "Who's the finance editor of the *Wall Street Journal?*" or "Is there a national organization of inventors?" most library reference departments will look up the answer for you on the phone. Call your library and ask for the reference department.

Bacon's Newspaper/Magazine Directory. 2 volumes. The newspaper volume offers names, addresses, and phone and fax numbers of daily and weekly newspapers in the U.S. and Canada, with names of section editors as well as lists of columnists and news syndicates. Daily papers are also indexed by "Area of Dominant Influence" (ADI), so that you can look up, say, Buffalo, New York, and find listed thirteen newspapers that serve the greater Buffalo area, in descending order of circulation. The magazine volume offers magazines, newsletters, and city/regional business tabloids indexed by subject classifications as well as alphabetically, with names of editors, addresses, and fax and phone numbers.

Bacon's Radio/TV/Cable Directory. 2 volumes. Fewer libraries carry this set than the Newspaper/Magazine set. Contains names, addresses, phone and fax numbers, and profiles of all U.S. radio and TV stations and about 400 cable stations as well as hosts, producers, and broadcast times for specific programs. Like the Newspaper/Magazine volumes, it has an "Area of Dominant Influence" index along with a subject index that allows you to look up, say, "business" or "health" and locate all the relevant shows. In 1994, each two-volume *Bacon's* set cost $270; call 1-800-621-0561 if you must have your own copy.

Broadcasting and Cable Yearbook. Geographical listings of all radio, TV, and cable stations in the U.S.; includes format, target audience, and name of programming director but not individual hosts/producers. Useful as a starting point for pitch letters or phone pitches; call the stations for names of people to pitch to.

Chase's Annual Events: The Day-by-Day Directory. Contains thousands of special days, weeks, months, and anniversaries to which you can tie your publicity, indexed by title and key words.

Directories in Print. A great source of information about reference works where you should plant free listings. If you're a consultant, for instance, more than half a dozen directories are listed that would probably give you free publicity. It includes special "buyers' guide" issues of magazines and membership directories of professional organizations.

Editor and Publisher International Yearbook. Lists daily and weekly newspapers, including military, black, gay and lesbian, ethnic, religious, and college newspapers, all with circulation figures, addresses, fax and phone numbers, and names of editors. It also lists foreign correspondents based in the U.S.

Encyclopedia of Associations. 3 volumes. Guide to nearly 23,000 national organizations, professional societies, trade groups, and interest groups, from the Aaron Burr Association to the ZZ Top International Fan Club, most publishing a newsletter or magazine for members; indexed alphabetically by topic, from aardvarks, to Zionism.

Gale Directory of Publications and Broadcast Media. 3 volumes. Geographic listings by state and city of weekly and daily newspapers, magazines, and radio and TV stations. Most periodical listings include editors' names; radio and TV entries are less useful, including the format (news, hit radio, country, etc.) but not names of program hosts or producers.

Literary Market Place. Every library worthy of the name owns this. It includes listings of publishers, freelance editors, ghostwriters, publishing consultants, literary agents, lecture agents, radio and TV programs that feature books, clipping bureaus, and writers' conferences.

Newsletters in Print. Full descriptions of well over 10,000 newsletters, with their frequency, size, price, circulation, and whether they accept article submissions. It has an unusually good subject index.

Oxbridge Directory of Newsletters. Complete contact information for more than 20,000 U.S. and Canadian newsletters, from *Apartment Law Insider* to *Zen Notes.* It states that newsletters constitute 30 percent of all publications.

Standard Periodical Directory. Very brief listings of more than 75,000 magazines, yearbooks, and directories published in the U.S. and Canada, with name of editor-in-chief and contact information. Since subject headings are extremely broad, you'd have to do a lot of searching and screening to use this for sending out press releases.

Standard Rate and Data Service. 2 volumes of special interest to "Six Steps" readers: Business Publications and Consumer Magazines. Incomplete listings designed for advertising placements, but helpful for PR placements, too. The Consumer Magazines volume includes categories like "bridal," "crafts," "sports," and "youth." Each listing gives a brief profile, editor's name, and complete contact information. Most ad agencies subscribe to SRDS, and may be happy to donate superseded issues to you rather than the dump.

Ulrich's International Periodicals Directory. 3 hefty volumes. Helpful if you want to publish something professional or academic to be read by, say, actuaries or zoologists. Has international scope, so you could send a release (if you should want to) to *Zhongguo Qiyejia (Chinese Entrepreneurs)* or *Saagverken (Sawmills,* published in Sweden). Start with the subject cross-index.

Working Press of the Nation. 4 volumes. Volume 1, Newspapers, offers section editors, circulation, deadlines, contact information for daily and weekly newspapers, as well as specialized, religious, black, and foreign-language newspapers in the U.S. Like *Bacon's* (see above), it has an ADI index. Volume 2, Magazines and Internal Publications, lists one editor, contact information, and freelance pay for more than 5,400 magazines and 2,500 company or association publications. Volume 3, Radio and TV Stations, lists stations geographically, by ADI, and by the subject focus of specific station programs, such as business, ecology, farm, music, sports, and travel. Highly recommended. Volume 4, Feature Writers, Photographers, and Professional Speakers, includes freelance writers listed by subject area, with enough information to facilitate schmoozing.

Books and Audiotapes

I've provided the ordering address for books and tapes that are more difficult to find in bookstores.

On Getting Media Publicity

Brown, Lillian, *Your Public Best* (New York: Newmarket Press, 1989). From the former chief TV makeup artist for CBS News, this book is especially slanted to the needs of political figures, but offers almost sixty pages of advice for anyone on dressing and making up for TV, along with tips on advanced challenges like using a TelePrompTer and surviving a media stakeout at your house.

Kotler, Philip, Irving Rein, and Martin Stoller, *High Visibility: The Professional Guide to Celebrity Marketing* (Stoneham, MA: Butterworth-Heinemann, 1990). An eye-opening quasi-academic study of the process of making and maintaining celebrityhood in entertainment, sports, politics, the professions, and other realms, including the role of coaches, managers, and the media, as well as the person aspiring to fame and his or her audience.

Kremer, John, *1001 Ways to Market Your Books* (Fairfield, IA: Open Horizons, 1990). For publishers and writers, includes zillions of ways to promote books, some offbeat. Revised and updated every few years.

Lant, Dr. Jeffrey, *The Unabashed Self-Promoter's Guide: What Every Man, Woman, Child and Organization in America Needs to Know About Getting Ahead by Exploiting the Media*, second edition (JLA Publications, P.O. Box 38-2767, Cambridge, MA 02238, 1992). The brash tone of this book is not to everyone's taste, but Lant includes dozens of helpful sample publicity documents and creative ideas. Very extensive list of media directories.

Parinello, Al, *On the Air: How to Get on Radio and TV Talk Shows and What to Do When You Get There* (Career Press,

P.O. Box 34, Hawthorne, NJ 07507, 1991). Delightful guide to doing your best on radio and TV talk shows by the cohost of *Your Own Success*, a syndicated radio show. Most valuable features: translations of studio hand signals, data on the top 100 broadcast markets, list of professions producers are wary of for guests, and addresses and phone numbers of top TV and radio talk shows.

Rochester, Larry, *Book Publicity for Authors and Publishers* (Sunset Hill Publishing, P.O. Box 444, Fall River Mills, CA 96028, 1992). With decades of experience as a talk show host and producer in radio and TV, Larry Rochester leads the reader through the steps of contacting radio and TV shows, keeping producers on your side, and remaining centered and professional amidst the chaos of a broadcast session. Occasionally laugh-out-loud funny; indispensable for anyone embarking on a multicity publicity tour.

Ryan, Charlotte, *Prime Time Activism* (Boston: South End Press, 1991). A fascinating treatise on the politics of newsworthiness. Highly recommended if you're trying to get publicity for a cause.

Schmertz, Herb, with William Novak, *Goodbye to the Low Profile: The Art of Creative Confrontation* (Boston: Little, Brown, 1986). If *60 Minutes* calls you, hold them off until you run to the library and borrow this book. Excellent advice for dealing with hostile media, from a Vice-President for Public Affairs at Mobil Oil.

Yale, David R., *The Publicity Handbook: How to Maximize Publicity for Products, Services and Organizations* (NTC Business Books, 4255 West Touhy Ave., Lincolnwood, IL 60646, 1991). Recommended for nonprofit organizations. Includes guidelines for press conferences, choosing and training spokespeople, and handling crisis situations, and useful checklists for all the basic strategies.

On Getting Published

Applebaum, Judith, *How to Get Happily Published*, fourth edition (New York: HarperCollins, 1992). Excellent overview of publishing options and procedures, and a persuasive argument for why all authors, whether published by prestigious publishers or by themselves, need to take an active role in promoting their books.

Bennett, Hal Zina, with Michael Larsen, *How to Write with a Collaborator* (Cincinnati, OH: Writer's Digest Books, 1988). If I've convinced you that getting your work into print makes sense but you know you lack the time or skill to write yourself, consult this book on the collaboration option. Contains sample collaboration agreements and a comprehensive overview of the benefits and pitfalls of cowriting.

Poynter, Dan, *The Self-Publishing Manual: How to Write, Print and Sell Your Own Book*, sixth edition (Para Publishing, P.O. Box 4232, Santa Barbara, CA 93140, 1991). With a computer and desktop publishing software, it's easier than ever to turn your ideas into a credibility-enhancing book. Poynter takes you through all the steps, from generating the contents of the book to getting it printed, promoting it, and then coping with being a published author.

Yudkin, Marcia, *Freelance Writing for Magazines and Newspapers: Breaking in Without Selling Out* (New York: HarperCollins, 1988). "Anyone who buys Ms. Yudkin's book can count on a huge return on his or her investment. I don't think I've ever read a dissection of my profession that was as thorough, as fair-minded and as full of genuinely helpful information."—C. Michael Curtis, Senior Editor, *Atlantic Monthly*.

Yudkin, Marcia, *So You Want to Write a Book* (Creative Ways, P.O. Box 1310, Boston, MA 02117, 1990). How to focus a book idea, present it convincingly, and get the attention of the editor or agent who's right for you. Three-cassette audiotape set, with easy-reference checklists and a sample proposal that won a book contract.

On Writing

Associated Press Stylebook and Libel Manual (Reading, MA: Addison-Wesley, 1992). Alphabetical directory to standardized spelling, usage, punctuation, etc., with special chapters on avoiding libel, respecting copyright, and using the Freedom of Information Act.

Strunk, William, Jr., and E. B. White, *The Elements of Style*, third edition (New York: Macmillan, 1979). This slim, timeless volume has tutored millions in clear, concise writing. Go thou and learn likewise!

Venolia, Jan, *Rewrite Right! How to Revise Your Way to Better Writing* (Berkeley, CA: Ten Speed Press, 1987). Highly recommended handbook for editing your own press releases, tip sheets, and articles. Advice on cutting out jargon, clichés, and sexist language, and on putting in the commas, apostrophes, and capital letters that the media expect.

Zinsser, William, *On Writing Well: An Informal Guide to Writing Nonfiction*, fifth edition (New York: HarperCollins, 1994). Readable, wise guidance from a master craftsman: "A clear sentence is no accident. Very few sentences come out right the first time, or even the third time. Remember this as consolation in moments of despair." Part One alone, on basic principles of good nonfiction writing, is worth the price of the book.

On Speaking

Schloff, Laurie, and Marcia Yudkin, *Smart Speaking* (New York: Plume, 1991.) A problem-solving guide to communicating effectively in more than 100 situations, from calling people you don't know to speaking to an audience to coping with poor listeners.

Shenson, Howard L., *How to Develop and Promote Successful Seminars and Workshops* (New York: John Wiley, 1990). This amazingly detailed book explains more than you probably imagined there was to know about designing, scheduling, pricing, advertising, and promoting public seminars.

Walters, Dottie, and Lillet Walters, *Speak and Grow Rich* (New York: Prentice Hall, 1989). Solid overview of the speaking industry, by the longtime owner of a speaking bureau.

Newsletters

I recommend all of the following newsletters, which focus at least partly on do-it-yourself promotion and publicity. Unlike books, which you can read once, enjoy, and forget, newsletters provide reminders, information, and inspiration when they show up in your mailbox four, six, or twelve times per year. Send a self-addressed stamped envelope to the listed addresses for current subscription information.

The Art of Self-Promotion (Ilise Benun, editor), P.O. Box 23, Hoboken, NJ 07030. Quarterly.

The Creative Glow: How to Become More Inspired, Original and Productive in Your Work (Marcia Yudkin, editor), P.O. Box 1310, Boston, MA 02117. Bimonthly.

Guerrilla Marketing Newsletter (Jay Levinson, editor), P.O. Box 1336, Mill Valley, CA 94942. Bimonthly.

National Home Business Report (Barbara Brabec, editor), P.O. Box 2137, Naperville, IL 60567. Quarterly.

Winning Ways: The Unabashedly Positive Newsletter for Self-Bossers (Barbara Winter, editor), P.O. Box 39412, Minneapolis, MN 55439. Bimonthly.

Working from Home (Allan Cohen, editor), P.O. Box 1722, Hallandale, FL 33008. Monthly.

Affordable Publicity Resources

Please contact suppliers for current price and shipping information.

ABC Pictures. 1867 E. Florida St., Springfield, MO 65803 (417)869-9433. A wholesale source of inexpensive glossy lithographed photos appropriate for inclusion in press kits. In 1993, for example, 500 8″ × 10″ black-and-white head shots cost just $70.

America's Largest Newspapers. Abalone Press, 14 Hickory Ave., Takoma Park, MD 20912 (301)270-4524. The most inexpensive listings on disk that I know of. For the U.S.'s 150 largest newspapers, contains addresses, phone numbers, and names of editors of Food, Travel, Books, Health, Business, OpEd, Features, Home, Environment, Sports, Outdoor, Computers/Technology, and Arts and Entertainment sections. In 1993, it cost $34.99; available on either IBM-compatible or Macintosh disks.

Guide to Literary Agents and Art/Photo Reps. Writer's Digest Books, Cincinnati, OH. Annual directory of literary agents who can place a book manuscript with a publisher, divided into those who charge up-front fees and those who charge only commissions, and indexed by the kind of material they are willing to consider. Available in most bookstores that have a "Writing" section.

Marketing Made Easier: Guide to Free Product Publicity. Todd Publications, 18 North Greenbush Rd., West Nyack, NY 10994 (800)747-1056. Offers listings of more than 1,000 magazines, newsletters, and trade publications that accept press releases, indexed by subject, such as apparel, appliances, automotive, beverages, and so on. In 1993, this large-format book cost $25.

PR Profitcenter. Ad-Lib Publications, 51-½ West Adams, Fairfield, IA 52556 (800)669-0773. If you want names and addresses of magazine editors or radio or TV talk show producers *on disk* for a mass mailing, this is the most inexpensive source I know of. In 1993 you could buy the whole database of 4,000 magazine editors, 3,900 newspaper editors, and 3,500 radio/TV producers for just $150, or almost any selected portion of the database for a smaller price.

Publicity and Promotions Engagement Calendar. Open Horizons, P.O. Box 205, Fairfield, IA 52556 (515)472-6130. In an 8-½" by 11" calendar format, provides more than 1,850 special months, weeks, days, and anniversaries to which you could tie your publicity. Unlike *Chase's Annual Events*, described above and in Chapter 2, this is not indexed, but the 1993 edition cost only $9.95.

Radio–TV Interview Report. Bradley Communications Corp., 135 East Plumstead Ave., Box 1206, Lansdowne, PA 19050 (800)989-1400. Virtually everyone I know who's been listed here felt they more than got their money's worth of radio interviews. In 1993, a one-time half-page ad that went out to about 4,000 radio and TV hosts cost $325, including help coming up with an angle that makes sense for radio/TV. Most of those listed are book authors—suggest that your publisher pay.

Writer's Market. Writer's Digest Books. Indispensable resource if you want to write for magazines. Lists thousands of consumer and trade magazines, with contact information, pay rates, and kinds of material each publication seeks, in subject areas ranging from advertising to women's magazines. Its list of book publishers is too spotty to be of much help. Widely available in bookstores; the 1994 edition cost $26.95.

Yearbook of Experts, Authorities and Spokespersons. Broadcast Interview Source, 2233 Wisconsin Ave., NW, Washington, DC 10007 (800)955-0311. When a hot story breaks and *Nightline* needs an expert or the *Chicago Tribune* needs an expert to quote in the next twenty minutes, here's one of the books the media pull off the shelf. For the 1994 edition, a listing would have set you back just $245.00, including being indexed by nine topic words or phrases of your choice.

Professional Organizations

International Women's Writing Guild. Caller Box 810, Gracie Station, New York, NY 10028 (212)737-7536. Newsletter and conferences that help women connect with a collaborator or ghostwriter, freelance writers, or someone willing to coach you to the professional exposure you want.

National Speakers Association. 1500 S. Priest Drive, Tempe, AZ 85281 (602)968-2552. Professional education and networking; more than thirty local chapters throughout the U.S. and Canada.

National Writers Union. 873 Broadway, Suite 203, New York, NY 10003 (212)254-0279. Agitates for better working conditions for writers, represents writers in grievances against publishers; professional education and networking.

Public Relations Society of America. 33 Irving Place, New York, NY 10003 (212)995-2230. Organization for professional PR people, with more than 100 local chapters.

Toastmasters International. P.O. Box 9052, Mission Viejo, CA 92690 (714)858-8255. Structured program of mutual aid in becoming better speakers; speaking contests and awards; 7,200 local chapters throughout the world.

Women in Communications. 2101 Wilson Boulevard, Suite 417, Arlington, VA 22201 (703)528-4200. Professional organization for women in all branches of journalism.

CHAPTER 24

Beyond *Six Steps*

Creativity is indispensable, not only to obtain publicity but also to keep clients or customers satisfied, deal with financial challenges, and evolve a comfortable working routine—even to recognize new business opportunities right under your nose.

That's why I launched a newsletter called *The Creative Glow: How to Become More Inspired, Original and Productive in Your Work.* For $49, it delivers stimulating advice, inspiring examples, helpful resources, and easy-to-digest information on the latest research on creative excellence, six times per year. Every other month, receive a wealth of suggestions that will make your work more impressive and fulfilling, whether you're an abuse counselor or a zipper designer, an accountant or a zookeeper—or still hunting for your optimal career. Learn surprising new ways to beat procrastination, recover from burnout, tune in to the inspirations flitting through you all the time, find more time to do what you most enjoy, and get more done well by knowing how to work with rather than against your creative quirks. And this investment in your success and satisfaction carries no risk at all. You may receive a complete refund after your first issue if you don't agree that it's fun to read, informative, and motivating.

To order a newsletter subscription or learn more about audiotapes, videotapes, seminars, speaking services, editing by fax, or consulting on your publicity program or other writing projects, call Creative Ways at (800)898-3546 or (617)266-1613, or write to Marcia Yudkin at Creative Ways, P.O. Box 1310, Boston, MA 02117.

(That was all in good taste, wasn't it?)

Index